Expanded Secor

In Jesus' Wor

The Bringers of Hope

All New Messages from Jesus Today

To All of Humanity

Dec 12, 2020 – Mar 17, 2021

Key Life Lessons on Our Challenges of Today

The New Jesus Chronicles, *Book 3*

Representing the Masters of Wisdom of all Earth's History

Charol Messenger

The Bringers of Hope

In Jesus' Words, Today: Expanded Second Edition

Key Life Lessons on Our Challenges of Today

ISBN: 979- 8521465880

Messenger Publishing, Denver, Colorado
AwakeningKeys.com CharolMessenger.com

Cover image: "Gentle Spirit - ethereal golden light," ID 525125932, Artist Nikki Zalewski, signed model release with Shutterstock, Inc., standard license.
Cover design: NZGraphics.com

Your Awakening Attitude of Service: In Jesus' Words, Today (2020) and it's prequel *In Jesus' Words, Today: Humanity's Magnificent Future* (1st edition 2019) are acclaimed in the nationwide news media release Oct 21, 2020, with over 1,500 Google searches day one. *"I am so grateful that the news of these two books was picked up by NBC News!"*

In Jesus' Words, Today: Humanity's Magnificent Future is published in paperback and Kindle and as an audiobook on Audible with a male narrator as Jesus. In this Expanded Second Edition, Volume I is All New Messages from Jesus. Volume II is the original and *complete* three-part collection of Letters from Jesus and is the 2019 book that was honored by Dr. Marilyn Todman, CEO of Preach the Word Worldwide Network TV, at their annual Shining Stars Gala; plus to two global TV interviews December 2019.

Charol Messenger's writings have been compared to those of Neale Donald Walsch, Eckhart Tolle, James Redfield, Gina Lake, and David R. Hawkins.

A *spiritual revealer* attuned to the undercurrent hum sweeping through humanity today, visionary Charol Messenger's sixteen book awards in nondenominational spirituality include six international First Place and Second Place. She is an Honoree of Marquis Who's Who in America 2020.

Reviews

"It is refreshing to hear what Jesus is saying to us today. Thank you, Charol, for being a blessed vessel for Jesus. You have a special touch from Him." - **Dr. Marilyn Todman, CEO Preach the Word Worldwide Network TV**

"Lovingly empowering message from Jesus 2,000 years later." 5 stars. "Humanity has evolved since Jesus was with us in human form and so has his message to us. He lovingly encourages us to look for the hidden divinity within and see through the illusion of isolation. There is so much hope and praise in his words that it feels much easier to do. Besides, the Ascended Masters who walked the Earth with us have done it, so why can't we, when we too have the spark of God within us? The assurance that Good will prevail and that life on Earth is evolving into a more compassionate expression is coming strongly through this book. This is so uplifting and comforting. I'm very grateful to Charol that she has enabled Jesus to come back and be with us again." – **Michael Matik, London UK, Reiki Master, Remote Healer** under the guidance of Archangel Michael. Author of *Become Your Higher Self: Experience Fast Spiritual Awakening,* free at awakeningkey.com and becomehigherself.com.
Facebook admin facebook.com/groups/becomehigherself. Founder of Become Higher Self Mentors & Healers, who volunteer services, remotely and globally. Contact Michael@awakeningkey.com.

"Exquisite! I was humbled to tears, the words reaching into my soul! The voice in this book is so clearly of Jesus. The 'voice' fills you up with strength and love. There is a gentle power in it, and it lifts you up. I felt a trusted authority in the tone, a caring instructor." - **Claudia Watts Edge, IANDS Conference host, public speaker and radio guest as NDE experiencer; author of *Gifts from the Edge:*** *Stories of the Other Side* and *Lessons from the Other Side,* and ***We Touched Heaven*** (2021) **endorsed by Raymond A. Moody, PhD. M.D.** ClaudiaEdge.com

"I LOVED THIS BOOK! A NON-RELIGIOUS RELATIONSHIP WITH JESUS. THE WORDS WERE SO WARM AND INVITING, I JUST CURLED UP AND LISTENED TO HIS WORDS, MY BROTHER'S WORDS, MY SOUL REMEMBERING HIM. THE WORLD NEEDS TO REMEMBER HIM, AND HE CAN BE FOUND IN THIS BOOK." – **Seeker (Dec 11, 2019, 5 Stars)**

"A guide for lightworkers who are lost in today's dark world. So many people I know are crying out from the depths of their hearts. The world seems so dark, and we sense our old structures crumbling. We feel like there is something important we should be doing, but we aren't sure where to start. Here is the most beautiful book. It is a guide for lightworkers in a time of enormous transformation of nations and individuals: 'We of the Council of Light are reaching out to the multitudes. We bring strength. We bring support. We change hearts and minds. Those who prefer destruction are facing their final days, of this you can be sure. Thus, believe in the good of humanity.' In this beautiful channeling, Jesus and the Council of Light reveal a plan to fully restore the original intention for humanity. Just when we feel all hope is lost...... My heart and mind are bathed in the beautiful light of this book." - **Amiee Laun (Audiobook on Audible, Feb 16, 2020, 5 Stars)**

"A map to our buried spiritual selves. I was awed by this profound book, but soon realized that Charol Messenger had provided us with a spiritual resource unlike any other. It's for anyone who feels alone in the world and unheard, who seeks inspiration and peace within. These are Jesus' words, as told to Charol, words of truth and enlightenment." - **Barbara Munson, co-author** of historical biography *Gilly: A Humble Crusader,* owner Munson Communications **(Feb 3, 2020, 5 Stars)**

Fifteen reviews 2020 on Goodreads.com

goodreads.com/book/show/50030666-in-jesus-words-today

Jul 18 Kiersten Bray 5 Stars ~ This book is an important reminder for us to stay present, be awake, and to seek the guidance of Spirit, God, and the angels. Furthermore, Jesus also wants to impart to the rest of us that there are methods on how to be Awake and Attentive. This is important because I have a busy schedule, and to have these tips as a reminder helps me to come back to that relaxed state of the mind and body. Jesus shared these ancient teachings of meditation:

- To be still in the body.
- To quieten the mind through rhythmic breathing.
- To slow the thoughts gently and without rushing.
- To quieten our emotions by allowing the peace to fill us.
- To let go of all around us until we are only in the moment.
- To surrender our personal choices to the divine will within us.
- To be still in that gentle, kind surrender only to the good.
- To allow our feelings to relax and our mind to flow.

Do you feel the connection to this? Well, if you do, practice this as much as you practice being kind, loving, and helpful to others. This is the message of this book, and we will find that if we follow it, we can truly walk on the Earth, happy and victorious.

Jul 18 Mckayla Green 5 Stars ~ May God Bless You, Charol Messenger! This book is what is truly needed to help others see themselves as powerful, skilled, and divine. Not a lot of us understand what we can do to become victorious and succeed in the mission that God has set for us. This book has sought to change that, it has empowered me, and it has made me aware of what I can do to give what I have to others. Knowing this is something of a blessing. It gives me the confidence to continue sharing what I have to my family, my friends, and the rest of the world! I've always felt the need to write my own books because I am in love with life, culture, and the study of religion. I know that Jesus' message is true, and it is what God wants us to do and wants me to do for myself and others. Anyone reading this book will slowly become aware of what they can do to contribute to the world. Keep on writing great books, Charol. You inspire me!

Jul 21 Leonardo Charles 5 Stars ~ God created the world so that we can co-create, explore our gifts, and depend on one another. It is high time that we know this truth. There are some of us not fully comprehending it. However, Jesus wrote this book, through Charol, so we know there are already lightworkers assigned by God to lead and teach us how to live. Peace, joy, and love are what we need so that we can become rich in our lives! This is the message of this book, and we must take this message with absolute attention and focus. We can use the ancient practices of meditation so that we can live this truth, should we fall short because of our weaknesses. This is one of the best books to read if you want to change your life! Feel it, take it seriously, and practice the teachings with due diligence. You will find that life is rich, after all!

Jul 21 Betty Nelson 5 Stars ~ Witnessing the message of this book and allowing it to transcend me was enriching for me. I have already felt the calling from God to live out my life from his guidance, and I know that I can only live it if I practice his words and teachings. Reading this book has confirmed my understanding of what God truly wants from His people. I give full credit to Charol because, without her book from Jesus, I might still feel disempowered to begin my spiritual journey and my calling, but with his help, I'm now becoming confident that this is what I need to do. Each one of us can offer something profound and meaningful. Jesus calls it lightworkers or teachers, and I believe that to be the same. We all teach, connect, and collaborate with others so that we can make this world a great place for all!

Jul 19 Lana Mora 5 Stars ~ Develop the wisdom on living in love and kindness from Jesus' words. Charol made sure to write her communion with God so that it would inspire and motivate all of humanity in this new millennium. Many of us live God's words, and Jesus is reaching out so that we can become lightworkers like the angels that God sent before. This book teaches us how to be faithful in our calling and how to be strong to live in kindness, peace, and without judgment. Similar to the Bible, there are teachings passed on here as well; moreover, the message that comes from Jesus in the 21st Century becomes even more direct and intentional. Jesus makes sure to let us know how we can live God's vision, and that is from the state of being that is love, compassion, and kindness. Thank you so much, Charol, for sending us this beautiful message from Jesus that will hopefully change the course of our lives!

Jul 18 Tiffany Potts 5 Stars ~ Learning about God on a deeper level is what this is all about. The Bible is great, but to have that interpreted from the Spirit speaks more in-depth. Knowing Jesus' words in the 21st Century made me aware that I am special. I have this gift to develop and reach out to many. We are all lightworkers, and for us to use that skill, we need to meditate, do things with love, and to be at peace. This message from Jesus is moving, and it is also effective if done correctly. The deep meditation techniques should be done in a quiet place, and then make sure to feel the power of these teachings, embrace them with all your heart, and listen to the silence around you. If you practice this, you can hear Jesus' message. Anyone reading it will be a servant to the world and live in peace and harmony with everyone! Thank you for this amazing and inspiring message!

Jul 19 Gracelyn Cooke 5 Stars ~ Rekindling what I've lost in my soul! The story about a boy in this book brought tears to my eyes. I feel so much a connection to it. I believe that each one of us has this dark side in our life that, no matter what we do, will influence our connection with others. As the story of the boy began to taunt me, Jesus made sure to let me know that even if I might be hurt from my past and present experiences, I am still required to give love wherever and whenever. To give love will heal you, and to share that with all living beings is what we are here for. Heal, love, and offer help was what I learned from this story. This book is something I highly recommend to everyone! It's time to use our SOUL to connect to others, use Jesus' words to live our lives, and create from our God-given skills to help others. Read this and live in God's truth!

Jul 19 Nyla Christensen 5 Stars ~ Wholeness, Love, Divinity, and Light Workers. These are some of the topics I grasped from this book. I loved this topic because it made me aware of what I set out to do in my life and for humanity. Wholeness is an important topic because I want the whole of myself to reach out to others. Wholeness can also only be grasped and lived out if we heal. The story of the girl in this book taught me that. After healing comes divinity. And once we feel the sacredness of our soul, we then offer our life for the benefit of others. Knowing this gives us power and encouragement. To live a life that is guided by God is the way to live in peace, bliss, and joy. Thank you for sharing Jesus' words, Charol!

Sep 25 Greg Clark 5 Stars ~ I love how spiritual the book is and how it can change people's lives. Wise words, Charol!

Jul 21 Aidan Andersen 5 Stars ~ Evolved thinking, evolved humans! This is what I learned and I will forever be grateful for this book. I've always known that life is not what it seems to be in the concept of form and structure. I have known that there is something deeper, something profound, and something unbeknownst to many. So, when I came across this book, my thoughts were confirmed. Reading this book is highly influential to the mind. Having this as your guide provides that strength in the soul to overcome whatever obstacles that life throws at us, so that we will realize our true nature and our true power, and that is soul and love. Read this book if you want to feel a miraculous transformation in your BEING. Hats off! Most moving and inspiring!

Jul 21 Paisley Booker 5 Stars ~ This book is bright, fascinating, and profound.. Jesus spoke through Charol in ways that we all need to hear in the 21st Century. People may be losing hope, but Jesus wants us to know that we needn't. In contrast, he wants us to know that the world is changing. So, if you're feeling hopeless, uninspired, confused, and failing in your life goals, read this book and be surprised at what it will teach you! Thank you, Charol! May Jesus speak to you more so that you may continue blessing others with his words.

Sep 25 Emma Wells 5 Stars ~ Jesus spoke through Charol in ways that we all need to hear in the 21st Century. Thank you, Charol!

Jul 21 Derick Ware 5 Stars ~ How to live in a state of Grace? Consciousness is a huge topic, and we begin to know about that from the first chapter of this book. Knowing what consciousness means is power and cultivating the practice on how to be conscious is first before anything can fall into place. That is why Jesus is teaching us, through Charol, that love, nonjudgment and compassion for others are equally important. When we practice this, we can become more conscious. Similarly, teaching the readers how to meditate also is one of the best techniques to reach a level of consciousness that is like how Jesus connected to his own inner being, which is God. So, if you feel that calling in your soul to revive and become more of who you are, and less of who you think you are, give this book a shot and practice Jesus' teachings!

Jul 21 Maribel Jefferson 5 Stars ~ To be victorious in life is to be victorious from our soul first, and that is by becoming more conscious. But what is consciousness? Consciousness is our waking state that we know how powerful we truly are. But how does one become conscious? Well, Jesus teaches us that and so many other ways to BE. This book is amazing and is truly a work of the Lord! I love how spiritual the book is and how it can change people's lives. The Bible is an awesome tool, and when someone interprets its words, such as Charol, it connects even more deeply with the readers. It is time we heal and then use our talents to serve others. Read this book and be overcome by miracles. Thank you for these wise words, Charol!

Jul 17 PrincesPoole 5 Stars ~ Consciousness, God, and Soul! These are three of the topics that we are all trying to grasp but fail to comprehend. Why? As people, we look at these topics as a contradiction to how we should live in the mind and how we should constitutionalize our life. Knowing God, and that deep connection to our Soul, we have something so powerful that we can live the life we have always envisioned to live. Moreover, living in consciousness doesn't only mean living your desired life; it also means using your God-given skills to serve and help others. Reading this book will change the world because it will change every one of us to live in how God planned our lives to be. There is no greater glory than to be called upon to greatness so that we can co-create with others. This book teaches us how to be that. To listen, to breathe deeply into our existence, and to live in harmony with God. Thank you for your thoughtful message, Charol! This is inspiring!

Jul 17 Bobby Salinas 5 Stars ~ This book gives me hope! It makes me hopeful that I can change my current circumstances and make them better. I had an unpleasant experience in my life as a child, and I want to forget that. With this message of healing, peace and meditation, I am slowly becoming more open to practicing these in my life. We all wish a good life—a peaceful one, in fact, and it is time to give this to myself. So, if you are looking to heal and find out what God has planned, this is a great book to read. This is relevant in all of our lives right now because of the pandemic. People losing their jobs, feeling isolated, and feeling like the world might reach an end. But there is hope, and you'll find this message to be true if you take everything here to heart.

Jul 17 Jonathon Summers 5 Stars ~ Spirituality is different from religion. Jesus' words are so enriching, and will teach the readers how to be victorious in the elements of love, compassion, and helpfulness. We are here to enjoy what God has created. There is more to life than what appears to be, and you will hear all the secrets that life has to offer. Charol is one of the best authors in the world of Spirit. She knows how to communicate her information that will move the hearts of others. We already know this truth in our hearts but reading about it takes us back to our true nature. Get this book if you are ready to evolve into your higher self. Feel the calling and go deep into your growth.

Dearest friends, I am returned.

In your heart, I reach across the dimensions of life to speak to you, to guide you, to show you the way.

Everyone on the planet is being visited by a Teaching angel. I have prepared the way for the Teaching angels to open each heart. For this *is* the time long foretold and, though it is at times forbearing, it is also the jewel of humanity's long journey.

You are *now* arising into the Intended souls you always were meant to be.

CONTENTS

Volume I

New Letters from Jesus, 2021

Key Life Lessons on Our Challenges of Today

Volume II

Letters from Jesus, 2019

Improved

(in First Edition, this is Vol I)

Part I
The Days Long Foretold

Part II
Return of All the Saints

Part III
There Once Was a Girl

Appendices

The Messenger

I first talked to God when I was three years old, in my backyard, speaking up to the heavens. I remember a sunny day with clouds.

Jesus brings to us today hopeful new messages, writing through Charol Messenger who transcribes from the "still small voice within."

It began November 2, 1975 at 2:00 a.m. when Charol was shaken out of her mundane life. After a harrowing week, turning to prayer for help, she fell into a deep slumber, in which she saw angels surrounding her amidst a heavenly glow, heard their chorus of song outside the Gates of Heaven, and felt the presence of Archangel Michael overlighting her as revelations came in waves to her about humanity's future. The next day, she began writing.

After further profound events 1982-1989, 1994, 2011-2017—on January 13, 2019 at 3:30 a.m., Charol was wakened by an inner nudging and went to her meditation room. In the arm chair, while she was deep in the consciousness, Jesus began speaking to her the first Letter of many that he wishes to share with all humanity. Enveloped in his loving energy, feeling his grace and tenderness and inimitable Presence, she wrote down the words.

In this series IN JESUS' WORDS, TODAY, Jesus is writing in his own voice and point of view. He also authored all of the previous Messenger books and blogs, which Charol received as her Higher Consciousness.

My eternal gratitude to my dearest friend Barbara Munson for her irreplaceable support and friendship.

Especially, I owe everything to Jesus – who has guided my every Higher step.

Volume I

New Letters from Jesus, 2021

To *All* of Humanity
Whoever you are, wherever you are
All races and all peoples,
Whether you follow a faith, or have none

December 12, 2020 – March 17, 2021

Key Life Lessons on Our Challenges of Today

Jesus representing the Council of Light, the Masters of Wisdom of the Spiritual Hierarchy

We are all connected.

We are one.

Just as all the cells in the body comprise the body

and as all the droplets in the seas comprise the sea.

Introduction

December 16, 2020

Dearest ones, I am not asking you to be Christian or to follow any religion at all.

I am sharing with you ideals to live by—for a peaceful life, in which mutual respect is the path, and honor and integrity are the daily guide.

I speak to you not as a Master of all.

I speak to you only as an elder brother who wants for you to be at peace, in your heart, in your mind, and in your daily life.

I am your brother. And you may ask for my counsel and emotional support at any time. I am always here for you.

I love you. I truly do. I am called Jesus. But you may call me Brother.

I am speaking to you today as one of the Ascended Masters, representing all of the saints and great spiritual Teachers from all of Earth's history.

For today humanity cries out, *Help me!*

And we all hear you.

And we are *all* here—now—with you.

Blessing you.

I am your brother, eternally, Jesus-Sananda.

1.
The Bringers of Hope

December 12, 2020

Hello, dearest friends. Tidings and great joy.

In your sorrow of the tragic year 2020, I speak to you of a picture not too far ahead when all of humanity will find your balance—in kindness and courage, in goodwill and compassion.

The world over, people are in grief over losing a loved one to the Covid-19 disease of the body.

Many are also in grief and in desperate sadness at the disease of the loss of goodwill in some people's hearts.

Many in the world, in many lands, are in a desperate desire to be looked upon as equals, not as despicable human beings . . . because of their color or heritage.

The greatest sadness for humanity is the horrible cruelty inflicted upon peoples of other races and cultures. This is a tragedy more horrific than even the Covid-19 disease of the body.

The disease of malice is more unconscionable than the Covid-19 virus that has devastated millions upon millions.

I must take a moment to say that America is at a crucial turning point.

Will the majority—who *do* believe in compassion for all—stand up for the innate principle of the innate dignity of *every* human being?

For *this* is the challenge, and *this* is America's greatest challenge.

Will you live with an open heart toward all who are different from you, and an open mind toward all you do not yet understand, *and* stand up for what is right for the greater good of all?

For *this* is the test of this Time:

The struggle to keep democracy, for all the world and peoples in all lands. It is the right of *every* person, of every race, color, and ancestry to have the same opportunities as every other person.

This is the test of this Time.

My beloved friends, I speak to *all* peoples. I speak to *every* heart.

I—once Jesus of Nazareth—am once again among you. Now. Today.

My *Light* was born in awakening my reason, my vision, and my compassion—to embrace *every* other.

Dearest one, come into my arms. Let me hold you.

In this *Light,* which we all are when in our pure intentions, we are born anew.

In this *Light,* I hold you—dearest one, whoever you are.

In this *Light,* I enfold you with the pure compassion of an unbiased Love.

For I Love you just as you are. And I enfold you now in the *Light* of grace, the *Light* of strength in the purpose you have before you, the *Light* of tolerance, and the *Light* of an unbiased heart.

Dearest one, take my hand, I counsel you.

Take my hand, I guide you.

Take my hand, I show you what to do and how to do it.

For you, my dear, are in the embrace of *The Divine Light* which counsels all of your ways.

Dearest, *you* are the hope of the world, through your deepest wishes to be a helpful and supportive presence.

You are the hope of the world, through your persistence in pursuing your dreams.

Because you see what is wrong, and you see what needs to be done. And, in this, I am with you. I and all the Counselors of Heaven. I and all the angels of all time. I am with you.

In your heart.

Because you also are able to know *The Divine,* which has shown you already every step to take—for your own greater good and for the greater good of all humanity.

Live your life with this one goal: *I serve the greater good.*

In this attitude: You will have peace in your mind. You will have the strength of angels. You will have the wisdom of the saints. You will have the clear inner understanding that is awakened when your heart arrives into *this* moment:

I live to help others, for all of my days.

When this awakens in your heart—*then* you are a bringer of hope to all. Then you are a lamp of Insight that others may see the way.

Then, my dear friend, *then* you are my ally and, in all that you do, I am with you. And, in all that you do, you are a *Light* of hope for the world.

Because hope is the greatest gift to humanity, and it is born *through* wise actions, strong endurance, a lasting commitment, and an open mind.

You, my dear friend, are in this life, at this time, to bring HOPE in all that you do . . . in all that you dream.

I am your beloved, with you now. I and all the saints of all the Ages. I and all the Masters of all the Ages. We are *here,* now. In the world, to guide the way.

I am eternally called Sananda. You may call me Jesus, as I was and am the same.

And I have now arisen, to show the way, to bear *The Light*. That all will feel the blessed gift . . . of an open heart.

And so it is.

I AM

2.
Humanity Is Now in Phase Two

December 13, 2020

Dearest ones, I bring you tidings of great joy.

First, let me say that I and all the Masters of Light and all the angels grieve for your sorrow and your hardship.

As I and all the Masters have lived on Earth, we understand the desolation and the terrible losses that you now bear.

Now, in our Full Light—here with you and among you, to guide, counsel, and even heal—we are also able to see beyond this moment, even beyond these centuries: to the future of humanity, on this Earth.

So know this:

All that you are having to endure will pass away. And what awaits humanity is a healthier world, and a more peaceful and tolerant world.

It is coming. But it is not yet.

However, dearest friends, be assured:

Humanity already *has* crossed the threshold from the worst of diseases (of body and of mind) and the worst of atrocities upon others. And, now, humanity has stepped into the first days of a new Era, which bodes increased well-being, increased goodwill, and increased tolerance toward others who are different.

In this new world—now already entered, evidenced by the bright young minds and giving hearts—humanity *now* begins Phase Two of the unfolding of the higher Insights, higher understanding, the greater capacity to love and forgive, and the greater capacity to see solutions to the physical ailments of the physical world.

You are, just now, embarking upon the intended life for all of humanity: To live as equals with the angels—in conscience, in the strength of goodwill, and in the generosity of spirit.

So, although all of you worldwide are still struggling to live your best Natures and to keep hope alive—I am here TODAY to tell you:

Keep HOPE alive. Keep LOVING and forgiving.

For *this* is how you change the world TODAY for yourself *and* for future generations.

This is your calling, dear one: To serve others.
Live your dreams and your visions.
In this, grace is yours.

Now, about this enduring time. The effects and preponderance of lingering health problems from the Covid-19 virus WILL subside, will lessen. It does take a while—until after the masses, worldwide, have been vaccinated (yes) to about 70 percent of the population. (This may take about four years. If it is less, that is possible, but I am seeing this for the world as a whole.)

Please do trust in SCIENCE, as this is the effect of minds enlightened with higher reasoning. And when guided by *compassionate reason,* all good things flow forth.

Let your Counsel within from *The Divine* be your assurance.

However, keeping in mind that it might be four years more (once on the vaccines) to eradicate the danger, please practice caution. I say this with love.

As to another desperate social problem, worldwide, I also bring hope:

Dark hearts who entice others to danger or harm, or who threaten others, or imprison others, or oppress and dominate others: This is NOW a just cause—to stand for the freedom *and* equality of *all* peoples, of *all* races, in *all* lands.

Stand for freedom. That is a Divine birthright of *every* person, every female, every child, every male.

This Darkness is fear of *The Light,* and fear of any other person who is self-endowed.

The Divine does NOT favor one race over any other. *The Divine Source of All Life* equally endows every female, every child, every male with the innate ability to directly communicate with God and the angels, and the innate ability to be filled with higher reason, higher knowing, and the capacity to love and value *all* peoples, as well as all animals and the earth and seas.

During this Darkness, many illumined new minds have a great sensibility and open hearts. They are able to see the *Light* in others, to heal the darkness where it resides. They are able to Lift Up others into the soul consciousness of the Higher Self. They are also gifted visionaries with technological advances to heal the problems of this world: through science, medicine, and social justice for all.

Dearest ones, I write of these matters—as I represent the Council of Light, the Masters of Wisdom, the saints and angels—not only because this Dark Time is the reported Tribulation. But mostly to assure you that it is *not* forever.

And that even in the midst of this great abuse by many toward those who are unlike them—there is *now,* already, a Rising Tide toward the freedom of all.

And in this Rising Tide of goodwill toward all—in all lands—is born a new strength of spirit that *all* have the right to live equally: under The Law of God. And that any effort, by *any* person(s), will be repudiated, without fail.

Dearest ones, I speak of this because your souls cry out for reason. Your souls cry out for fairness. Your souls cry out for social equality. — And *that* is social justice, now a Rising Tide, the world across.

And soon a Tsunami.

For freedom and kindness are innately endowed, to all.

I am your brother, Jesus. Also named, eternally, Sananda.

I am your friend forever, and I am with you always—no matter who you are, or where you are, and no matter the faith you follow or if you have none.

For the Love of God is not bound by faith. It is *free* to every heart, and speaks within as *the still small voice within.*

And so it is, always was, and always will be.

Yours eternally, Jesus-Sananda.

3.

The Awakening Time

December 14, 2020

Dearest ones, in the beginning, *all* were pure beings of *Light*. There was only *The Divine Light*—from which *all* became self-endowed.

In the beginning, life was *The Force of Goodness* and *all* beings were what you call angels.

These original beings of *The Light* were without count, multitudes upon multitudes. And they existed in a joy of the heart (or soul), and they reveled in splendorous play and sensitivity and caring for all the others.

This Perfection you call Heaven.

Then some of the angels, in their joyous creativity and curiosity, devised worlds; then upon these worlds, the human being—or physical incarnations of the Perfect Beings.

In the beginning all was pure joy. And the worlds were without count, in a multitude of dimensions.

In the third dimension came the first of the incarnated angels. They enjoyed the new experiences, the colors, the textures, the sights, the sounds. The perfection of creation.

This was the first world created. It was called Perona, and existed in what you call the Pleiades.

In this first world, in their delight, some of the angels grew enamored with their creative abilities . . . and devised the other worlds.

Then they traveled to these other worlds, in the many dimensions.

In the third dimension, they first traveled to Orion, Sirius, Andromeda, and Polaris (the "North Star").

It was eons upon eons before they came to Earth.

This jewel of the universes stole their hearts. This perfect world was so intoxicating in its beauty that many of the angels chose to remain here—and to live out physical lives in their perfect physical bodies.

And they are still here.

Over the eons and eons, some of these angels found their way back to their higher wisdom (the Home Awareness). But many did not.

Many of these who are still incarnating on this Earth are now filled with the Higher Awareness and are recalling the pure heart and attitude—which is compassion for all creatures.

Many of those who are currently incarnated on this Earth are, however, *not* in their higher Insight and are deluged by whims, fancies, and grievances. These are today the minority of humans on this Earth; but, as before on Perona, in their grievance they are a forceful influence.

So, dear friends to whom I am writing *today,* as your own heart is touched by the words in my new teachings (such as in this book), and you recognize that *you* wish to be a healing and helpful influence in this world—*you* are an awakened angel.

As an awakened angel, you are now endowed with the current of *The Living Source of All Life,* through which you are able to be a source of comfort, directly, to any who suffers (human and animal). And you are also able to even bring physical relief, likely even restorative relief.

This is one of your many gifts.

Why do I tell you this?

Because, dear friend, in life—especially in this world, *especially* now—you are needed: To give the Insights that come into your awakened mind. To give the nurturing that comes into your awakened heart.

For to restore this humanity, to awaken the Pure Light that is in all, your task is to live freely in your talents. Let your *Light* be your voice. Let your *Light* be your service. Let your *Light* be the counsel of your days.

In this way, you kindle you own expansion in the innate powers—only as a force for good. In this way, you are a part of the *sparking* to awakening of all those who do not yet see the way.

Dearest one, as an awakened angel—as an awakened *Light Source*—you are one of the many, and you are not alone.

It is your task, now, in this life—to live fully to lift others up.

How?

Give them hope.

Hope opens their hearts. Hope softens their wounds. Hope erases their despair.

For all wrongdoing is born out of despair.

Offer hope and you are bringing *Light* to this world.

And it is time.

This is The Awakening Time. For the multitudes. And all the hardships, all the distress, are Hope seeking its way into people's hearts.

You are here, now, to be a bringer of *Light*. And *The Light* is given through bringing hope.

And know this:

In all that you do for the peace of this world, I am with you. I and all the Masters of Wisdom. I and all the angels of the Heavens.

We are with you—in this splendorous time on planet Earth, for the uplifting of all humanity . . . to the *Light* within.

In your words, in your gifts, in your talents—you are a bringer of *Light*. A bringer of hope.

Blessed be.

I am forever Jesus-Sananda.

4.
The Awakened Heart

December 16, 2020

Hello, dearest friends. I am here to encourage you, to show you a world healed . . . of the pandemic *and* of the racial prejudice that darkens *The Light* of the intended human race.

First, I give you my blessing. For on this day and all the days ahead—*you* are a new person, with a new sense of your place in the world and a new idea of why you are here.

This life is your best life—of *all* the many many lives you have lived. Hundreds on this Earth. Thousands before. And, yes, I speak of being in a human body.

So what makes *this* life exceptional? *Why* is this very difficult life the best of all?

It is because *now* you see, you feel, you anticipate, you envision. It is because *now* you live not for yourself alone. *Now* you recognize that you are in this life not only for yourself—but for *all* around you. *All* peoples, of *all* races. And all animals. *And* the earth and seas.

In *this* life—more than any other before—you SEE. You FEEL. You KNOW:

I am here to serve.

This is the calling.
This is the purpose.
This is the intended life.

As to the healing:

Beyond the immediate danger of the Covid-19 pandemic (four years globally, on the vaccine), people relax. There is an ease. There is a joy. Laughter, singing, and dancing.

Relief.

At long last.

There is still a need for vaccinations beyond that time. Diseases remain in the earth for a very long time.

But by four years from now (on the vaccine), the deadly threat, globally, is behind you.

Until then, dear ones, be wise. Because your family needs you. And I need you . . . as a voice of optimism on planet Earth.

Yes, there is a reason for optimism.

Racial strife is a sad commentary on any society.

Yet as it is deeply born, in many nations, it is a seed to uproot.

Love does not judge.

Love does not hinder.

Love does not fear.

Fear not those who look different than you.

Embrace them.

They are your brothers. They are your sisters.

Fear not those who see God in a different way than you do.

God is the same in every heart.

The Masters of Wisdom from all of Earth's history teach love . . . tolerance . . . forgiveness . . . patience.

They wish for all of us on Earth (and beyond) to embrace the beauty of the soul . . . which is visible on the face and in the actions.

Walk with each other in appreciation of the *Light* within. *That* is the *Original Flame* given to *every* person.

Every person on Earth was born with this innate Connection with *The Divine* (by whatever name you give it).

For all of you—and all of us—were born with The Divine Spark in us.

And *every* one of us Awakens to this when we see beyond ourselves and see—truly see and value—every other life in the world around us.

For *that* is how we Awaken to the Divinity already there within us.

And once we do—we are changed forever.

You now feel this burgeoning *Light* and Knowing waking up.

As you allow yourself to feel the growing abundant joy spilling forth from the center of Divine Truth within you, from that day forward, more and more, you are becoming a Light Being in service to the inborn *Light* in every other.

For this is who you were born to be.

And *this* is the life of your Awakening.

This is the firm foundation of how—over time, exponentially—every human comes to see that life is a gift . . . to be shared . . . in all of its potential bounty.

And you, dear friend, are one of these . . . in service to *The Light*—which is The Awakened Heart.

And in all that you do, in service to *The Light* and Love, I am with you, as your counselor and your guide.

As are all the Masters of Wisdom, also *now* fully embodied . . . right now . . . on planet Earth. Among you. With you. Loving you.

I am eternally Jesus-Sananda.

Blessed be.

5.

Your Purpose

December 17, 2020

Hello, dearest friends. I have an encouraging lesson for you.

You were born to be a healer—to heal sorrow, to heal despair, to heal what ails the soul.

This is your purpose.

Whatever gifts you have—your talents, aptitudes, abilities—these are *your* work in the world . . . and are also the processes and situations through which you serve the downtrodden.

For you—as you are—are able to see, and understand, the scope and breadth of destitution. Even if this is not your own experience, in your empathy you can see and comprehend the challenges of those who do.

Thus, when I say you were born a healer—I mean of all those conditions in life where one suffers.

This, I say, as a wake-up call to you—that *You* are needed.

Yes, a job is necessary . . . and is a means by which to give. But in addition to whatever work you are drawn to, you also have the personal responsibility to ease others' despair.

This can be a personal commitment, whether through your work or as a volunteer.

Just know this: Your personal values show on your face and in your actions. So know that your every behavior, interaction, and choices are you expressing what matters most to you.

So, even in your job—whatever it is; and even in your play; and especially in relationships or encounters with others—keep in mind: You are your values.

So value courtesy. Value respect. Value integrity. For these are the measure of a person.

And when these are what matter to you, you help others—by improving their lives . . . and helping them to feel at peace.

And *this* is how you are a blessing in the world.

I am your brother, Jesus-Sananda. And you may simply call me brother.

Always . . . I am here for you. Always.

6.

Your Soul Gift

December 18, 2020

Hello, dearest ones. Today, I acknowledge every one of you for your open heart toward others.

For this is your gift to *Life* in this life.

You are in this life to be an example of Goodwill. This is your strength—and this is your Nature.

As a representative of *The Good,* which you are, you help others to realize that they too have unique sensibilities—and that that is okay. Not only okay . . . but remarkable.

In this—your Strength—is the innate ability to see others' *Light,* no matter who they are . . . or how horrible.

This matters, because when people are horrible . . . though it is just to hold them accountable for their cruelty, at the same time you can send *LIGHT* to them, to their hearts, their conscience (however dim), and even their souls.

For in their horrible attitudes and actions, harming others, though they do not say this out loud: They live in terror in every instant. They live in fear of retribution. They live in desolate isolation . . . because they feel abandoned.

And, yes, they do this to themselves. And, yes, they will face retribution (in this life, through their inner torment; in other lives, until they make correction in their biases and blame; and in the afterlife, also until they realize that their hardness is merely their fear of being unloved).

And so, though you are right to hold them accountable to the harm they do, at the same time by sending *LIGHT* to their hearts, to surround them until they let it in, you are helping them as souls who have not yet let go of feeling inadequate. Yes, they have caused great and grievous harm. Yes, they will face an accounting. And, yes, they suffer from their own flaws in how they treat others.

But, dear *Light,* let *LIGHT* be your Soul Gift to the ones who are lost in the horrible attitudes. Let *LIGHT* be the gift of *The Soul* to the souls.

Do this, for your own heart's healing. And in this, they receive (unconsciously, in the soul awareness) the spiritual Spark they need to have the Dawning Realization (eventually, in this life or another) that their fears have imprisoned and punished not others—but themselves.

Thus, when someone at last comes to the Dawning Realization, *that* is a step toward softening the heart and a step toward *discovering* the gentler life . . . through a heart beginning to accept that there is another way.

I now let you go, dear one, to meditate on this: How to be reasonable in the justice system, while also (silently and in your own heart) sending *LIGHT* so that those ones at some time will come to the Dawning Realization of an easier life: to love one another, no matter who one is, or where; no matter the level of forgiveness, no matter the level of the open heart.

For dearest—we are *all* in *The Life* together. And we *all* need one another.

Your brother, forever, I am Jesus-Sananda.

7.
The Way Forward

December 19, 2020

Hello, dearest ones. I bring you hope.

I know this has been a very difficult time for you, and I am so sorry for your losses and struggles.

I can only say that, in this difficult time, in your heart I am with you . . . as an inner comfort and to offer solace.

Your strength is in your ability to see all peoples as friends. Your strength is in opening your heart to the love of God, which brings an inner calm.

I am your brother, always. In this way, my voice is in your heart.

Let me also show you the way forward.

You are seeing a new answer for your dilemma. You are finding new ideas to bridge the gulf. And, in this, safety.

Answers, remedies, and resolve are NOW en route to you.

I see healing in the distressing situations.

I see remedies offered—SOON.

I see compliance where there has been none.

And in the months ahead, I see an open door—to all of you, all of humanity. A doorway to a better understanding of how to repair not only bodies but judgments, not only pain but biases.

The months ahead bring more appreciation . . . and more tolerance.

For there has been unbridled hostility unleashed—and . . .

> Now it is reined in.
> Now it is measured.
> Now it is contained.
> Now it is no longer free to do harm.[1]

Because NOW is a time to heal—bodies and burdens.

Now is a time to repair—hatred and rigidity.

Now is a time to find balance and to restore equanimity.

---

[1] See post January 8, 2021, volume I chapter 19.

And, in this, I am heard. For I—and all the angels—are bestowing the inner quiet upon the troubled hearts and minds.

And in the inner quiet, balance is restored.

For in the inner quiet is the calming influence.

In the inner quiet is the easy breath.

In the inner quiet is the stillness, wherein peace resides.

Thus, dearest one, go into your own inner quiet—through the easy breath—and allow peace to bathe you, body and soul.

In your heart, I am with you always.

I am your brother, Jesus-Sananda.

8.

Your Soul Grace

December 20, 2020

Dearest ones, all will be will.

Be at peace. In time, the Covid-19 pandemic will be under control, worldwide.

In time, racial justice will be a fair and respectful way of life, including in America.

This *does* require generations more, I am sorry.

But know this, new leaders are showing the way. And acceptance *will* become the way of life, in time.

Until then, live with courtesy toward those who are unlike you.

For know this:

The soul of every one is pure *Light.*

Live by your own soul's *Light,* and live by perceiving the *Light* that *is* in every other, and you will be a part of transforming the global society to more dignity in how others are treated.

For God sees all as divine. *Every* soul is innately a gift of life to all of humanity. The human race has many forms. The soul is only Grace.

Live by your grace—and you will be in gentility and in respect. As you also wish to be treated.

This is the single rule of a peaceful life. And I am with you, in your heart and in your aspirations.

I too am SOUL.

And as I awakened to *The Divine* within, so can you. So can all.

For *this* is the journey . . . of all souls. Of each and every one.

And any bias is only the face of fear.

Live in your Grace and you will always know the right actions and right thoughts—which *are The Divine* living through you.

The Divine life is GRACE.

I am your brother, with you in joy and in loss.
Holding you.
Guiding you.
Forever.
No matter who you are, where you are, or how you live.
I am in the moments you are lost and in the moments you live by Grace.
And so it is.

Your brother, Jesus-Sananda.

9.

The Light Expands

December 21, 2020

Hello, dearest ones. On this day, *The Light* expands . . . across the world.

Today, hearts are filled with hope . . . and a vision of how to give hope to others.

Today, minds are illuminated with new Insights on the purpose of life:

To be helpful to others

Today, you can begin a new path . . . toward more open hearts, in all lands.

Today, trust the inner knowing that is assuring you. This *is* the path, and this *is* the time.

For today life renews, again. Life renews . . . and you as well.

I am your beloved brother always, Jesus-Sananda.

10.

An Open Heart

December 22, 2020

Dearest ones, this day brings hope—for all of humanity.

Restoration of norms is in sight. Healing of the body from the pandemic is in sight.

You are also renewing your faith in humanity. And this is the greatest growth of all.

For your faith in the human spirit—which is innately divine—is the single best outcome of this horrible tragedy in the physical challenges of the Covid-19 virus.

So, to now have a renewed faith in humanity's selfless spirit is the greatest healing there is. For it is your faith in your goodwill that is your *Living Light.*

It is your faith in your selfless generosity—of spirit—that is showing you your inner strength and fortitude.

It is your faith in yourself that is opening Insights into who you really are: an open heart.

You now can see how gracious you are, how gentle you are.

You now can see all that you cherish—what you cherish most—is your love for those in your life: your family, your friends, your special allies and spiritual alliances . . . and your beloved pets.

For some of you, your pet—a cherished dog, or cat, or rabbit, or guinea pig, or even a chicken, a horse, a mule, or a cow; any of God's creatures—for some of you, your pet is your most beloved friend.

And in the trials of this year, when so much has stressed you, when so much has been lost—or fear of loss, or fear of impending loss of what will you do now—for some of you, that single animal, or person, is the anchor of love who fills your heart the most deeply.

It is that single animal, or person, to whom you give your full trust and all of your compassion.

And dearest one, that is enough for you to *know* that you are loved . . . and that love is all that matters.

For when everything in your life is threatened, and you don't know where you will live or sleep, or you don't know if you are safe, or what you will eat today—the love you feel for your pet or that one person is enough for you to know, in your depth, that:

> You are enough. You are okay. *And* you *will* be okay.
> Help is coming.
> People really do care.
> You will be okay.

It is this that opens your trust—in others and in yourself.
It is this that opens your heart . . . to possibilities.
And it is possibilities that give you hope.
And it is *hope* that keeps your inner flame burning and your inner *Light* alive.

In hope, you find that you do know you are going to be okay.
In hope, you feel it is okay to trust, again.
In hope, you look up, you look out. You stand up, you stand out. You reach up, you reach out.
In hope, you find your way.

Because with hope alive in your heart—once again you are empowered . . . with love.
Love for yourself. Love for others.
And *this* is the day that you now open your heart . . . and hope again.
And *this* is the day that life finds you . . . and life gives to you . . . the assurance and the inner strength, that:

> You are okay . . .
> and *we* need you.
> We need *you*.
>
> Will you now join with us in helping others in need?
> For you are the *Light* and love that others need.
> Will you now stand with us?
> Will you now walk with us?
> Will you now join with us in bringing help to others?

And today, dear friend, today—*this* is the day you find your own joy, your own peace, your own comfort.
In comforting others.

I am your beloved brother, with you in this life and through this journey.

I am your brother, holding you and counseling you—within, through *the still small voice within.*

Blessed are you.

And thank you, dear soul, for hearing me and feeling me in your heart. For there, we walk together all of your days.

I am Jesus, once of Nazareth, eternally named Sananda.

The Elder Brother.

11.
The Years Ahead

December 23, 2020

Hello, dearest ones.

We of the Spiritual Hierarchy recommend today that you look to the Star of the Heavens for your encouragement. Although this astronomical alignment of the planets Jupiter and Saturn is a rare event (800 years since they were close to each other)—it is merely a precursor of a better life ahead for you. Not in a magical way. In a symbolic way.

The years ahead globally are still difficult—financially, health, racial equity, and religious tolerance.

However, incrementally there is an expansion of reason and compassion, particularly as the threat of the disease Covid-19 subsides.

Thus, we encourage you to remain confident . . . and surely persistent in your vision of improving life for others. For it is your vision that helps to bring a Restoration of generosity, in all nations.

And it is this generous nature that rebuilds hope for the future, for the masses.

Thus, we can announce that the next seven years (2021-2027), while still hard, are a ladder climbing up—as if to the stars—toward more kindness in the whole of you.

For keep in mind, it matters little what the few angry souls do. But it matters immensely—transformatively—what the majority of you do.

And *that* is the masses, worldwide.

And that is *You.*

For you are one of those who is carrying an open heart.

And *this* is how you change the world.

I am Jesus-Sananda, representing the Spiritual Hierarchy, the Council of Light.

12.

A New Year's Message, Which Begins December 25

December 25, 2020

Hello, dearest ones.

Today is the birth of a renewed compassion for others.

For in this time when you are focused on giving, your heart is open to sharing and you are more forgiving.

Dearest ones, let *this* be the tone of this new year. For *this* is the tone of love and thoughtfulness.

Today begins your new year.

Let *this* be your new beginning.

And in every breath you take, think of this life with gratitude. With every breath you take, love someone else.

For the breath of life is compassion and, without either, you are not the full Self you were born to be.

Thus, today I wish you the Breath of Life, which is love.

I am your brother, Jesus-Sananda.

13.

When In Your Own Higher Consciousness

December 26, 2020

The Universal Consciousness is your connection to *The All That Is,* or as some people call this MIND, God.

You are born with this spark of The Divine Connection already in you.

And it is this spark that awakens in you when your heart is open to freely loving others, without bias.

Dearest ones, the Universal I AM *is* your own higher consciousness—which activates when you personally ascend into your own sense of wellness in the soul. And this is achieved when you release your need for perfection in the world and seek only to provide sustenance to any other who needs it.

For The Divine Connection is born in an attitude of respect of The Life Force, in all of its forms—all humans, all animals, and even the Earth itself.

For *all* of life is created out of the love of God. And however you define God or define love, the actions of creating anything are You emulating the inborn instinctive nature of what God is: Love.

For God is not only Love because the Bible says it is so. That scholar had learned this truth:

That the fabric of all life is the force of good that is called Love;

That the force of life that binds all existence. and that is the *glue* of all that is manifest, is Love;

And that without this inherent force of consciousness—which is all and is everything—there would be no Love and there would be no thing . . . nothing.

For *all* that exists—in all worlds, all dimension, all time; and before all worlds, all dimensions, and all time—is the *force* called Love . . . which *is* Mind . . . which is consciousness . . . which is called God, by many names.

Thus, when it is said that without love you have nothing, that means that without Love there is nothing; that without Love, nothing would exist.

For God *is* Love . . . is consciousness . . . *is* the glue of all life, of *all* that exists—before, now, and after.

God is Love, is Consciousness.

The fabric of life—of the Universe—*is* Love, is Consciousness.

Thus, you too are born in—and out of—Love.

For Love is all that is, ever was, ever will be.

What you *feel* is Love—that pure sense of wonder that fills you to overflowing—that is You, the real You.

For You *are* Love.

And when your heart is touched, and a light awakens within you, by whatever name you call it—you are then able to hear God, the angels, and the Masters, those who lived and taught in previous Ages.

And, then, all you care about is to help others, in their everyday lives. Because your own heart is awakened and you are filled with only and wholly—Love.

And this is the gift I bring to you now. To stir not your mind—but your heart.

For the secret to life, to peace, is an open heart.

Because *that* is the Love you have sought. And that is the Love that then immerses you. Because, then, Love is all you are.

Blessings, dear one. From this day forward, all you are is Love.

I am your brother, Jesus-Sananda, representing the Spiritual Hierarchy, the Council of Light, who are the Masters of all Earth's history . . . and beyond.

In this current Age (Aquarius), we are all with you, and among you—to guide you—as you walk a new path . . . of love for all.

And so it is.

Blessed be.

14.

In Your Selfless Help to Others

December 27, 2020

Hello, my brothers and sisters. I honor you today for your open hearts and selfless natures.

Today you give yourself in the service of your fellows who are in need of comfort. You are gifting them in their times of need, and this is a calling of the soul.

For this—in all of your moments, in this endeavor and in your own needs—know that I am with you, I and all the angels who work with you and through you, and all the ascended masters who guide you and counsel you. What you do today and each day henceforth, in the name of *The Divine,* and the human need of those seeking your help, is a calling of the soul. And, for this, you are supported and have our respect. For, in this, you live the full Self that you are.

So, dearest, have a blessed moment, a blessed hour, a blessed year and a blessed life, and *know* that you have the gratitude of every human you now help.

And that is the greatest calling there is:

To go forth each day with the intent
to help, to heal, and to console.

I am your brother, walking with you. I and the angels who work with you and through you. I and the ascended masters who guide and counsel you in these days.

It is a good life.

I am your brother, Jesus-Sananda.

15.

Who I Am: My Undiscovered Youth

December 30, 2020

Hello, dearest ones. I am with you forever. I am as near as your breath. I am in your thoughts. I am in your heart. I am in your dreams.

And now let me confirm who I am.

Yes, I am Jesus. Known as the Christ. Known as Jesus of Nazareth.

And I was born into a simple life to young Mary. And I was loved by my parents.

I did spend many years studying the ancient mysteries, with the Essenes, who still practice today; and in Nepal, the Himalayas, and upper India.

As a young man, I traveled extensively, learning the ways of the Masters and being taught by elders and sages.

I studied the *Mahabharata* of Hinduism (source of the *Bhagavad Gita)* and all the ancient records of the Eras before. I was schooled in languages, in the stars, and in the practical sciences—by scribes.

All of this is recorded in those ancient lands, in their histories, of the young man who traveled and came for a time.

I was very studious and loved learning. I was like a sponge and I couldn't soak it up fast enough.

I studied history, cultures, medicines, and practical ways to earn a living.

And then came the time when I was blessed. An angel came to me—in a vision—and said to me, "You are given this course of action. To give over your life in the service of humankind, that all men and women will know what you understand: That they are loved, by *The One God.* That they are in this world not to discard others, but to help others. That they can find understanding, and even wisdom, if they only listen to *The God Within . . .*"

And the angel said to me—whose name was and is The Archangel of All the Heavens, The Divine Light known by the Name of Gabriel—"So young Jesus, will you now forsake all the suffering in the world and rise up into your own *Light,* and speak of these things, for *The One God?"*

Humbled, I knelt, wept and, in rapture, looked up into the glorious *Light* that is The Archangel Gabriel and quietly said, "Yes."

"Then so it is," said The Angel. "Rise up and go forth and spread the word—that love is all there is. That if we but love one another, all of our suffering will disappear."

And I rose up. In the blessing. And began my journey.

Dearest ones, I add to my story (shared in my other books with Charol, as here in Volume II, which is the original First Edition of this book) to give you hope. Because what I learned that day—in *The Light* of The Angel—is that no matter how far we travel, how many books we read, or what we accomplish—there is only one thing we need to know and do in this life. And that is to love one another. And when we do that, deeply, clearly—to our core—all of our fears melt away and there is nothing we cannot do . . . when we are in the grace of *The One God,* which is *The Divine* within us. For there is no other God than *the inner love* that lives in our hearts.

All words, all beliefs are empty if not spoken in love.

For without love, we are nothing. And with love, all the world is only Light—*The Light* that guides us and shows us the way.

I speak to you, dear one, today simply to share what I have learned. Because this is the way to peace—in your heart, in your mind, in your actions.

Love of each other stills the disquiet and clears the kind and turbulent emotions.

Love of yourself, in this humility, heals all sorrow and shows you the strength that is in you.

So, dear one, will you now rise up and walk with me and *be* Love as an example in the world?

For this is why you were born. And this is your gift to all others.

Because all anyone really wants is to know love.

And when they feel it: They embrace it. They absorb it. They become it. And thereafter, they only live to serve.

This is the path of being patient, the path of living without hatred, the path of understanding others' pain and giving comfort.

And this is the path you now walk. And I am with you.

Your brother, Jesus-Sananda.

16.

The New Attitude Expanding

December 31, 2020

Hello, dearest ones. I know, you are thinking: At long last the end of 2020.

Yes, it was a very difficult period for all of you.

But I hope you realize, now, that it also was a period of awakening, in many ways.

You, dearest ones, have opened your hearts to each other in a bigger way than ever before.

You have opened your understanding and appreciation of people who look different than you, especially those whose hardships, for millennia, have hardened them.

Thus, you are more forgiving and tolerant than you have been.

At the same time, you are also more determined than ever before to right the wrongs, to fix the unfair public laws, to repair the injustice in the justice systems.

And *this* is the greatest awakening of all.

For, dear ones, when you are helping to open the rights of others who have been unjustly brutalized, you yourself are becoming of a healing mind.

For it is when you can embrace others who are unlike you that your own wounds are no longer all you think about.

And when you are doing this—you are a gift to the world.

Dearest ones, life is an opportunity to rise above injustices and to lift up others who have been wrongly disenfranchised. Life is an opportunity to lift up yourself out of "It's all about me" to "It's all about us.'"

This is the New Attitude that is now expanding across the world, in every land, in every pubic system.

This is the Age of Awakening.

And when people say awakening to what, that means awakening not to intellectual distractions—but to the *compassion* to see and feel not only others' pain . . . but others' value.

The Age of Awakening is singularly to see people—all peoples—as a part of *The Divine Consciousness* which is embodied in *every* person.

And this new Age is only just beginning.

Imagine what the future holds:
Loving as you are, as everyone is.
Born in *The Divine.*
Born *in* The Good.
Born good.
Born equal, all one and the same . . . in the soul.
This is who you are, dear one. This is who *everyone* is.

I am your brother, Jesus-Sananda. I am with you in all of your moments. All you need to do is call my name and I will be there, as the counsel in your heart.

Always.

Have a blessed year, dear one—through your open and forgiving spirit. For this is the you that I know. This is the you that I see.

This is who you are in your soul.

And I am with you, *in* the world and *in* your heart.

I am both in an embodied physical body—*now*—and still in the *Light of Ascension,* which is the journey of all the Ascended Masters and saints . . . and is also the path you are on.

This is the journey of discovering: *So this is what Love is? Wow.*

Yes, indeed. Wow.

Pure Love is the stuff of life . . . and is the purpose of life . . . and is *your* purpose.

17.

The Light of Days

January 1, 2021

And so, dear ones, here it is. A new year. A new breath. A new possibility.

In this, your renewed hope, courage, and conviction.

In this, your faithful persistence in seeing what is the best in humankind, seeing the qualities of generosity and kindness. — And being that yourself.

For that is all that matters as you proceed into The Light of Days. That is all that matters: hearts of goodwill.

For, in that, you find yourself . . . and you embrace others.

And, dear friends, that is the promise of this new year.

And in every look upon another, in every step you take toward healing the disquiet in this world, you walk with angels.

For know this:

Angels are abundantly in the world—*now*—with you and among you, angels who are still Their *Light*. Angels of The Divine Heavens, angels in their full Splendor, are round about you—*now*—in support and encouragement of all your good wishes for humanity.

So, dear one, live as the angel you once were—in The Beginning—and allow your Beloved Friends, who *still* Live in their full Splendor, to counsel you now.

For they *are* here. Multitudes. Not as humans. Not embodied. But as the pure *Light* that they are. As their Divine Wisdom that teaches *you* the purpose of All Life: To Love one another, without bias, with only an open heart.

For Love is all that matters. And Love is all there is.

I, with you, am your brother, Jesus-Sananda. And soon we will be speaking more about the Divine Beings of *Light* who are known as angels. Have a beautiful and hopeful new year. For hope is the salvation of all that you seek. Hope is the bearer of all that you render in the world. And I and the angels counsel you through *the still small voice within.*

18.

All Races Have Equal Capacity

January 2, 2021

Hello, dearest ones.

Let this new year be a focus of healing more than the body. Instead, focus on a healing of the riffs between the races.

All of humanity are of The One Source, *The Divine I AM.*

Every person is a physical representation of God, *The Divine.*

Not one race is superior to another.

All races have equal capacity to hear—and follow—*the still small voice within.*

And *every* person has the capacity to live in the higher Character from which *all* were born.

So, let this new year be your personal intention:

To love one another, seeing all as divine expressions of *The One Light,* which is called God.

I love you. I am your brother, Jesus-Sananda.

19.

Post the Insurrection of the American Capitol, Jan 6, 2021

January 8, 2021 – 9:09 a.m. MT

Hello, dearest ones, the fate of freedom is not lost. Freedom in America is not lost. This is not the end of democracy—in America, or in the world.

Democracy is strong. The majority of *all* peoples believe in humility and goodwill—which are the bedrock of free peoples.

So, dear ones, while this trial of terror is upsetting, please know that this is a clearing ground . . . of all that is not in the greater good.

This is a reminder of why it matters to care for others.

This is a reminder of why it matters to have elections and to choose *wise, sincere, good* people.

This is why it matters to see who is genuine and to *discern* who is not.

Fame is not the banner of freedom.

Ridicule and defamation are not regulations of elections—which is choices voiced.

Only honesty can be the regulator of elections—choices voiced.

Only humility can be the regulator of *how* to see and *how* to know who is honest and who is not.

This crisis in America is a turning point—toward *more* compassion . . . toward more caring . . . toward caring about what is the real character of those who are elected as "representatives" of the people.

For an honest character is not obsessed with attention . . . and is not a spewer of lies.

An honest character is only filled with a deep commitment to be of *service* and to help people have easier lives.

An honest character lives not for him or herself—but *only* to be of service.

An honest character is clearly evident by his or her words, actions, behaviors, and choices.

Trust only those people whose focus is not only on themselves.

And . . . you may be assured . . . that those who have wrought disaster (and still are) upon the peoples are, indeed, about to be disarmed.

Right is not might.

Right is justice . . . and justice is now at the door.

I am your beloved, Jesu-Sananda, always your friend.

20.

You Would Not Be in This Life If You Were Not Making a Difference, Already

February 2, 2021

Hello, dearest ones.

Today, I give you a glimpse into who you are, as humanity—so that you will see what I see.

I see a people who are imaginative. You are emboldened to give to others the beauty of life.

You are resilient in your love of life and all it offers.

You are generous with your goodwill, and fearless in the face of challenges.

You are brave and courageous in the face of obstacles and hardships.

You are kind and inventive in the face of cruelty.

You are always looking out for those you love, especially in the face of brutality and hatred.

Dearest friend, never doubt who you are.

You are my brother. You are my sister.

You are an heir of the angels who guide and counsel you.

You are in this life as a LIGHT of hope.

You are in this life as a BEACON of resilience . . . in ALL matters.

Dearest, know this:

You are in this life to give all that you are—your wisdom, your compassion, your creativity, your kindness—so that others will be filled with their own hope.

You are kin to *all* of humanity. *Every* person is your brother or sister. Every person seeks peace of mind. Every person seeks a quiet heart.

You are the *Light* of that gift to them. You are a voice of strength, confidence, and goodwill.

Believe in yourself. For you would not be in this life if you could not—and were not—making a difference already, right now. In this moment. On this day.

You would not still be here if you did not have more to give—for the good of all.

For that is YOUR life spark, your purpose, and your higher will.

And for this, I also can assure you:

You ARE, now, today, making people's lives better.

Also know this:

This world—and this nation America—is NOT at an impasse.

The struggle for goodwill as the marker of a good life is not the end all.

The good life is in the goodness that you see all around you, now.

Goodness surrounds you. Good people surround you.

Let *this* be your guide and your focus.

You, yourself, be that, too.

When you live to BE good in life—good shows you the way: to teach, to counsel . . . to heal . . . to build . . . to restore.

You are in this life TO HEAL and TO RESTORE the goodness that *every* heart seeks.

And where you do not see it is a soul in distress. And your STRENGTH is the counselor *within* you who *does* know how to HEAL those wounds and misguided aspirations.

For the only blame is in the one who chooses cruelty, not in the one who has not yet learned to heed The Inner Guide.

For The Inner Guide is the *only* voice of reason . . . and does *NOT* encourage hatred and does *not* feed fear.

You are THE HEALER. For kind counsel is found within a calm heart.

Of this, I encourage you to trust your own kind and gentle inner counsel *(not others who are bent on cruelty).*

Of this, I encourage you to heed the kind *inner guidance* that shows *how* to REPAIR distress and confusion.

In that is your Higher understanding.

Lastly:

Be fervent — but not audacious.

Be firm — but out of generosity.

Be strong — but out of the will to heal.

Never be so loud that you cannot hear *the still small voice within* that is the counsel and guidance of *The Divine,* and of myself, and of the angels.

For that voice is the "better angels" that guide you. And is never a voice of mis-counsel or misdirection.

The still small voice within is the true answer.
And if you do not hear it —

> Be still.
> Practice stillness.
> Daily.
> Until the *silence* is all there is.

And out of the deep *silence* comes *the still small voice within,* which is the Higher counsel.

I love you. I am your brother always, Jesus-Sananda.

21.

How Do You Know When It's the Right Decision?

March 11, 2021

Hello, my dearest. Today, we are opening the Veil to *all* of humanity.

You yourself very likely already are feeling a strong presence of loved ones. You yourself may already be seeing friends and family who have passed, in dreams, possibly in visions.

There is but a breath of distance between this world and the next. Because Earth is already in the *transcension* and is vibrating at a higher frequency than ever before.

Earth is already in a higher frequency.

This means that what looks like the third dimension is the world of only those who are lost in hatred and a fear of themselves, through which they abuse others around them.

This also means that the majority of humanity are *now* functioning emotionally and mentally in the *next* vibrational frequency, which is literally the fourth-dimension level of consciousness.

Then there are those whose abilities to live in the fullest breadth of the human spirit are functioning in the fifth-dimension frequency or level of consciousness. And this is those who are leaders in goodwill toward all. These are not only the young, but anyone whose purity of intention is the clearest and their entire focus of existence is to give of themselves to help others.

It matters not what are your talents or what you do. All that makes the difference—for your own genuine peace of mind—is to live in the *attitude* of helping others. When you do this—and this is your core value—all else that you do is through this lens.

This *attitude of service* is what heals your emotional wounds and alleviates your personal griefs and regrets. It is also what opens the path before you . . . so that you are drawn to those people and situations that bring to your awareness how *you* in particular can be a person of good in the world.

Dearest, your unique voice (your attitudes, beliefs, and comprehensions) are much needed in the world. For *you* are a part of a growing chorus.

This chorus is the heart songs of all awakening souls—not to sing the praises of God . . . but to *be* the voices of Divine Compassion and Reason in *all* that you do.

So dearest friend, trust in *the still small voice within* that prompts you to help. For this is I, and this is the angels who counsel you—and this is your own Conscience.

Let your conscience be your guide.

Now, if you are distraught over a decision you feel you have to make . . . perhaps it is because that is not the answer or action that is best in that circumstance, or in that moment. Perhaps your distress (and resistance) is your conscience saying: Not this. Perhaps your anguish over the decision or action is your conscience saying: Walk away.

Dearest, listen to your anxiety. Listen to your distress. Heed your own resistance to your own idea of what you think you need to do. For in your resistance is your answer.

If you are in great despair over what you think you have to do, *that* is your answer. Not this.

Listen to your heart. *Let your heart be your guide.*

So much in life is this choice. Do not go against your own heart's tugging.

If you are overwhelmed with agony—in the moment that you are taking a step toward an action you *think* you need to do—that is your soul saying: Not this.

In other words: Do this not.

In other words: *This* is not the choice. Walk away.

Dearest, life is all about choices, in every moment.

Go the way of your inexplicable but strong heart response and you will choose the path of peace, in your own heart—and *that* is *how* you can tell which way to go, what to do, and when.

If resisting the decision or choice: Stop. Do not proceed.

Your soul is saying: Not this.

If overwhelmed with an action you *think* you need to do, and you are distraught, your soul is saying: Not this. Walk away.

However, when you let go, when your mind is suddenly at ease and your heart is calm, and you feel a gentle quiet in yourself and a knowing—you then *can* know that you have made the right choice, for you.

Why do I talk of these things? Because life is full of these choices.

It is not even a matter of hearing *the still small voice within.*

It is even more obvious when you heed your strong emotions.

When distraught, or confused, or uncertain—the answer is: Do this not. Walk away.

For only the calm heart knows peace. And only the heart at peace can see the clear answer.

I love you. I am your brother, Jesus-Sananda.

22.

A Cure for Genetic Aging and Diseases Is on the Horizon

March 12, 2021

Hello, dearest ones. This day brings hope. For all that you have hoped for is *now* on your doorstep. This last year has been a desperate time, no matter where you are or who you are.

And now there is hope on the horizon of a way to overcome the devastation to your lives from the Covid-19 virus.

While a cure is not yet available—there *are,* now, enough means to manage the deadly infection. And *this* I and the Council of Light (Masters of all Earth's history) recommend that you do for yourself.

Trust the doctors. Trust the vaccines. Trust that this *is* the way out of the *darkness* that this virus has wrought.

In addition, I also can give you hopeful news about longevity. New scientific discoveries are—*now*—on the cusp of recognizing a genome that affects a person's aging process.

This means that the ailments of aging soon can be slowed down, by many years, from ten years to even twenty-five.

This means that one's inherent genetic makeup can be modified (by another generation) so that one's illnesses of aging can be delayed, slowed down, even minimized.

In addition, recognizing this genome can then be applied to other fatal and debilitating diseases, at all ages.

This *is* in the process of discovery. In time, perhaps another century, such treatments will become more adaptable.

This means that even childhood cancers can be eradicated.

Dearest one—you might even be one of those people helping in these discoveries. Which will help *all* of humanity.

If you feel a calling to cure a disease, or to be in a medical profession—follow this calling. For it takes many people, over many years, to do this.

Even so, we see that it is on the horizon, for *all* of humanity.

Blessings, dear one, in all that you do . . . for the greater good of all.

I am your brother, always. Jesus-Sananda.

23.

Your Attitude Is the Key

March 17, 2021

Hello, dearest friends. This day, I bring you hope. For this is the first day of a shift in the *attitudes* in humanity toward a common goal: to be whole, to be healthy, to be free of the Covid-19 virus.

Though the virus lingers, globally, this shift in *attitude* by the majority of peoples is the significant factor in moving humanity toward the elimination and management of this deadly virus, in its many forms.

Therefore, I can assure you that help is on the way. The scientists are industrious *and* persistent in waging this war against this disease.

Now, as to you. Let's change how we look at this.

How are you holding up? Are you taking care of your emotions, and your body? Are you finding a way to interact with family and loved ones?

In this very unusual time, the first global impact in a century, it is very important to find ways to lift your spirits.

This can be through meditation. Also through activities that stimulate the mind, aspirations, and physical wellness. Also through helping animals. And especially through helping people who cannot manage easily on their own.

For your own well-being, it is critical to find ways, daily, to raise your hope and optimism—*and* to encourage your gifting of your talents. For *this* is how you remain in harmony in your own mind and feelings.

When you are helping others, or are in situations that need your participation, you are lifting yourself also, out of the inclination to worry and despair.

So, finally, let me add: In this time of continuing challenges, your *attitude* is the key to how you remain hopeful in your own outcomes; such as with work, finances, security, a home, and sustenance. *Because* help *is* on the way.

And your open heart and enduring spirit are how *you* remain aware of *all* options. Keep an open mind. Be observant. Listen to the choices before you, and those that will be occurring to you. For help *is* all around you. And it is your own gifting that shows you the way.

All for now. Blessed be. I am forever your beloved brother Jesus-Sananda.

24.

The Harbingers of Self-Awareness

February 20, 2021

Dearest humanity, I am here with you. *In the world.* As are all the saints and Masters of all the Ages. Know that we are with you—and *among you.*

We are with you *now* because humanity is in an evolutionary leap—of self-awareness.

You are more conscious than you have ever been.

You are opening to the Universal Presence, which is Love.

You are expanding—*now*—into your own original sense of knowing what is best for the whole.

You are opening your mind to ideas of compassion, *and* reaching out to help others.

You, my friend, are *The New Humanity*. You are *The New Human.*

You, my friend, are one of the teachers of the Ages come to Earth at this time to teach by example:

That Love is the healer.

Love is the way.

Love is the example . . . for *all* that ails the world.

In this way, my dearly beloved, *you* are one of us: giving of yourself as a person of goodwill, without judgment toward any, with judgment toward none.

Yes, the world is filled with greater challenges—*now*—more than ever before. Yes, humanity is feeling torn between the old ways of fear and the new way of a generous heart. Yes, humanity is unleashing old shackles of falsehoods and mistrust, and is turning toward hope and kindness as the only way forward.

You, my dearly beloved, are in the world—*now*—because of *your* ability to see *how* to repair what has been broken (through despair, fear, and aggrandizement).

You, my friend, are in this world—*now*—because of your unique insights into *how* to heal peoples' wounds of the heart and mind and psyche—individually, but also the greater numbers.

Dearest, all that frightens people can be turned to the better *attitude*.
All that people suffer can be cured. Yes, cured.
All that people distrust can be brought into *The Light*—through *kindness*
All that people suffer in anger and outrage can be remedied.

And because of *your* natural abilities, *you* are one of the many now who is and will turn the tides of fear toward the common good.

And this is how the world goes on, and how humanity finds the better way: for the whole, for the good of all.

My dearest, this is your path. This is your talent. This is your gift to humanity. — No matter your age, no matter where you live, no matter your land, your nation, your race, your culture, your faith, or your past.

For *this* is the Age of *Conscience.*[2]

This is the Age of *Compassion.*

This is the Age of correcting all that has led peoples away from their *innate knowing* that life is meant to be lived in the *attitude* of *what is good for the whole.*

For by living *for the good of all,* hardships diminish . . . until they will fade away.

Anger is transformed by *hope.*

And you, my dearly beloved, *now live this*—by example.

Just focus on the greater good of all, and your own life will be a blessing and your own heart will be comforted.

For I am with you always.
Listen for *the still small voice within,* which is my counsel.
I lift you up.
I show you the way.

From there, on your own wings of confidence, you take flight . . . and you *know* just what to do—in the moment.

I love you. I am your brother. I am with you—*Now. In the world.*— And also as the Whole Ascended Being who is pure *Light* and pure awareness and pure knowing, *and* is also *present* and embodied.

---

[2] September 22, 2011 (autumnal equinox), we entered the new Cosmic Age, which lasts 26,500 years. This new Era is the "Age of Compassion." December 22, 2012 (winter solstice) was an explosion of consciousness. We have crossed the bridge. We have only just begun.

In this moment, I am a young man in form. Not born. But I have come as myself and I, too, am embracing all that you see around you in the world.

I speak softly and gently. Few know of me. But I am here.

I and all the saints and Masters of all the Ages, we are with you.

To lift you up.

To show you the way.

Until, in your own awakened self-knowing, you too take flight: in *goodwill toward all.*

I am yours forever, called Jesus of Nazareth. Eternally I am Sananda.

Volume II

Letters from Jesus, 2019

Improved

(the First Edition, updated)

Part I

The Days Long Foretold

New messages and meditations

January 13 – February 22, 2019

1

My Name Is Holy One

Dear one, I have risen.

You have called me brother over and over again. Let us now restore our companionship. For this is *your* strength in times of feeling out of control.

I now give you my hand in friendship, my brother. I clear the way for you in harmony, my sister. We are always together in spirit, and in flesh. I will not ever forsake you. I am with you always.

It is in Love that I am here with you today. Because you have called out, I have come. Let me be your Counselor. Let me struggle beside you. Let my voice be yours, in silence and in tumultuous times.

Dearest one, this is *now* an awakening time for you. You have journeyed a very far point in your unfolding, as you awaken to the extraordinary new vision: *"I am a balance of harmony in the world."*

May you cherish your talents and your true spirit of humility and goodwill. For this is the person you already are *and* came into this life to be.

You are *Light.* Your heart is full of love for the divinity in *every* creature and *every* person. In this way, peace is yours.

Blessings be with you on this day and every day hereafter. I am Sananda, once known as Jesus of Nazareth.

Received January 13, 2019, 3:30 a.m.

2
The Teaching Angels

Consciousness is born in all of us. It is who we really are.

Every person on the planet is awakening to a deeper understanding.

And everyone on the planet is now being visited by a Teaching angel.

These are those who awaken souls to who they truly are: eternal Selves, embarking now on a splendid new reality.

The Teaching angels are those who instruct souls in their sleep, about the universal principles that are magnifying at this time.

The Teaching angels speak into the hearts of those who are not yet aware of their greater purpose. They reveal the secrets of life and the reasons for existence in the physical.

For souls who are already on their higher path, the Teaching angels open the Heavens of Light and reveal the wisdoms of *All Knowing,* so that the novices will be impressed upon with sacred understanding and their spiritual duties in the world.

The Teaching angels are now a multitude, awakening *every* heart to your responsibilities as a sane and caring individual for those who are lost, those who wander without hope, and those who hurt themselves and others.

It is to this end that the *Angels of All Dimensions* now come to humanity. For humanity is *now* invoking its urgent plea:

- To understand the madness of some.
- To find a way to restore sanity in the lost.
- To awaken to their own higher dreams.

Because when you are actively serving the highest good of all, you are on your path of service. And this is how you know *why* you were born, *why* you are here, and what to do next.

Dearest soul, I Sananda (known as Jesus) have prepared the way for the Teaching angels to open each heart to wisdom and to bring the *awakened ones* to the doorstep of the new reality:

Which is now real.
Now solid.
Now manifest.

Live your higher Self and you will recognize that you are on a path not for yourself but for the whole. For this is the way to peace.

I bless you. I am with you.
Every day.
Every moment.
Listen *within.*

I am Sananda, once known as Jesus of Nazareth.

Received January 13, 2019, 3:30 a.m.

3
Humanity's Renewal

Now is the beginning of a world renewing, a world healing . . . *and* becoming its pure Intention.

The world is its peoples, the collective.

The world is also the creatures of the air, earth, and seas. And is the earth itself, is the waters, is the currents—which are the *breath*.

Now is the time. Humanity is awakening to its deeper understanding, that:

- *All* peoples are a part of the *Great Whole*.
- *All* peoples are a part of *The Great Consciousness*—which *is* Life itself.
- *All* peoples are worthy and are endowed with divinity.

Dearest souls:

- Forgive those who slight you, in their forgetting of who they are.
- Forgive those who kill, and your own heart will be free. Remember that souls awaken in their own time.
- Forgive those whose hearts are hardened, and your *own* heart will be clear and your worries absent.
- Forgive those who cause damage to others, and your *own* heart will be unencumbered.

These *are* the days long foretold, the days of the gnashing of teeth. And much is terrifying and much is sad.

This also is a time of humanity's renewal . . . and realignment toward your Intended state of being:

- To be filled with a kind heart.
- To have eyes that see all for what it is and see beyond what is obvious.
- To have ears that hear *The Divine* and the whisperings of angels.

Dearest souls, *this* is humanity's greatest Era ever.
Be not afraid. Be assured.
Because *you,* too, are one who feels the touch of God stirring within you.
You, too, feel my presence with you.
You, too, know the peace of trusting that every step you take is supported.

Dearest souls, I am with you, always.
Every day.
In each moment.
Hear me *within.*

I am *The Beloved I Am.* I am your befriender, known to humanity as the Christ, known to the awakened ones as the Beloved.
In the Home beyond, I am always Sananda.
Blessed be.

Received January 14, 2019

4
The Grand Creation

At this time, *The Divine Consciousness* is restoring humanity's original fulfillment:

That *you* are the awakened Beings of Light who came to Earth to discover the virtuous beauties of creation.

None of us began as physical forms. Every one of us was first *Light.* In that *Light,* we were full Beings, with delight in the magnificence of the origin of creation. We watched with awe as the forms took shape, the worlds of all sizes exploding with the power of life.

We watched with immense gratitude to *The One Mind* for the splendorous fulfillments of life forms: Earths of many colors. Earths of many levels of awareness. Earths *conscious* of being. Earths abundant. Levels of consciousness abundant: the tiniest of creatures, the most grand, even the most aware.

These Earths were born out of *The One Mind's* desire to create life in all manner of forms. From the microscopic to the most extraordinary.

Science, my dear souls, is the expression of *what is.* Science is the revealer, so that humans can remember who we all were in the beginning, before The Grand Creation.

You and I, Jesus-Sananda—every one of you and every one of human form—we *all* existed as Beings of Light *before* we ventured into form.

Some ventured at The Beginning, others over the eons. But *all* humans began in *The Origin Place* as Beings of Light.

Dearest friends, you are not lost, nor forgotten. You are exploring. For from The Origin, we all have explored. We explore what is, and wonder what is not. We explore what we know, and what we seek to know.

The nature of all conscious beings is to seek what we don't know, to discover. We are *all* discoverers, seeking to understand even more. Even though in The Origin as Beings of Light we knew all, we were even more interested in being fully expanded in understanding *all that is.*

Simply, know this:

You, my dearest, are in a human body only to be more of who you are and more of who you can be. Life is The Grand Creation, so that you are exploring all that might be.

It is time—*now*—dearest, to lift up your sight to the Heavens, from whence you came, and recall your Divine origin. Because when you remember the Whole You, the you who is filled with wonder, that is when you live it—here on Earth.

Life on Earth (as elsewhere) is changing, toward the original Intention: to be your blessed Self.

Give all that you are to this fulfillment, and you will be renewing and rekindling your innate Self, which is one of *The All.*

You are now exploring and seeking to understand. The discovery comes when you accept that you are, now, already the good you wish to be. All you need do is decide: Be your *Self,* the good one.

For when your heart is clear, all else becomes clear. And that is when you know, with humility and gratitude: *I also AM.*

Dearest one, I am with you in every moment. Listen for me, *within.*

I am your beloved, Jesus-Sananda.

Received January 15, 2019

5
The New Level of Consciousness

The time has come. The whole of the human race is *now* transcending into a *new* vibratory level of consciousness.

Yes, some are more attuned and are more endowed with the naturally instilled talents of generosity. However, the others, even though asleep in their inner nature, are *now* being taught in their sleep (as well as in their waking sleep). Thus, they, too, have now embarked upon a new way of experiencing the obstacles of life.

Dearest souls, we are all of *The Divine*. You are of *The Divine* and are able to be your full *Self*. Everyone can be the wise one. Everyone can be the selfless one.

It is who you are.

Do not look to others for *how* to do this. It is *inside* of you. You *already* are able to hear the angels speak to you. You *already* are able to know what is right to do, and what will cause you harm.

The secret to life is to accept this as real. Once you do, the whole is now available to you—and all the majesties of Heaven come to you to share with the others.

How is this possible?

Because once you have been reborn in your heart, and have bathed in the waters of new eyes and new ears, you are filled with grace and the grace of *The Divine* is bestowed upon you.

This is how you come to realize that The Majesties are real. You are, indeed, in the presence of those who imbue the sacred knowledge.

This, my dear, is all the assurance you need. For once your heart is open, you *feel* the grace of *The Blessed Ones* in your being and all around you. You feel their sweet breath, as a gentle breeze. You feel their sweet touch, as an angel's, upon you: upon your shoulders, to say, *Yes, I am with you.*

This is *The Divine Ones,* my dear.

This is the calm gratitude we have for you, for your deliberate and steady commitment to be helpful in the world. This is the quiet encouragement we speak into your thoughts, that you may be, forthwith, filled with the deepest compassion there is: For all others, whoever they are.

For, dearest ones, you *are* the Light of Heaven, *now*. And in this:

- We are your armor, against all that might seek to bring harm.
- We are your strength, that your body will be strong.
- We are the clear *knowing* that moves you with delight and awe.

Dearest ones, you are today reborn, in the Grace of all The Majesties who have gone before you. And in this, we are able to teach *through* you. And it is so.

I am your beloved, always with you. In gratitude, I am Jesus- Sananda.

Received January 16, 2019, six a.m.

6

The Jewel of Humanity's Long Journey

and When I Walked the Earth As Jesus of Nazareth

Hello, my dearest friends, this is a life of awakening. You are now realizing that all in this world is an experience to discover who you really are and how you best can be a giver.

All peoples in this world struggle. It is the way of the physical. However, changes are now ensuing. The vibration of life on Earth and, therefore, all in the world, is upleveling.

You are living in the *first transformation* of humanity, and life forms, since the beginning of physical existence. This means that as you become more imbued with your spiritual presence, you are immersing yourself in the *Light* of God—which is the *stuff* of life.

In the *Light* of God, you are being reborn.

Bathing in *this* Light—every molecule of your being, every atom, every cell—you are regenerating your body to its healthier state of being, *and* always awakening your Higher Mind (which functions *through* the physical brain).

It is true. *The Mind*—The Consciousness—is *not* the brain but is your eternal Self.

For all of us are *consciousness*—which is the *stuff* of thought, and which vibrates as love. The brain is the instrument *through which* the consciousness activates in physical reality.

Thus, my dearest, heal your mind by having a well body, which includes a brain that is not hindered. Be whole in body and you will be whole in mind.

Let me put it this way:

> When I walked the earth in the days as Jesus of Nazareth, I learned to respect all living forms and to appreciate the smallest of creatures. I learned to value every person, even the least of us. And I learned to be kind and humble in my days with those who tormented my body.
>
> This is how I was able to suffer in the flesh yet retain my better sensibility. For we all suffer when in the physical.

> Yet in our higher presence, we are able to lift our essence out of the suffering, so that it is not our prison.

Dearest one, whatever your condition on Earth, the best way to be free of suffering is to heal your own being. In this way, no matter what befalls you in the world, you are able to rise above it in your heart and mind.

I am writing to you these days because you and every other person in this world are *now* imbuing a higher *vibratory* frequency. While this may be intense at times for the body, it is also increasing your ability to perceive—and understand—all that is unseen by the physical eyes.

You, my friend, are drawn to teach others the simple *gratitude* that heals all wounds, inner and outer.

You, my friend, are *now* undergoing your own restoration of faith in *The All* and, thus, restoring faith in yourself.

As you relinquish the need to harbor ill will and to let go of resentment, you are healing your heart and mind of judgments, which make you ill.

As you hold yourself no higher than any other, and ask yourself why you are being forgiven by God, you are healing your body.

Dearest, the *secret to life* is to let go of fear, resentment, and judgment. For these create pain in the body, because they hold you down in the mire.

Emotions are the fuel. You either allow yourself to wallow in suffering—or you say, *"No, no more,"* and rise into your higher Self, which is full of *gratitude* for what you *do* have: a good heart.

Forgiveness heals your own potential to pain.

Forgiveness is the salve on your own wounds.

Allow yourself a generous nature, and you will release what has caused you distemper, in both body and mind.

This Era that you are now in is a very remarkable time and with challenges to faith.

To *retrain* and grow your wellness of spirit—thus your mind, then your body—live *every* day with hope.

> Seek hope.
> Be hope.
> Give hope.
> For *this* is *how* to traverse the anguish of the world.

I will speak more soon about this extraordinary life you are in. For this *is* the time long foretold and though it is, at times, forbearing it is also the jewel of humanity's long journey.

You are *now* arising into the Intended souls you always were meant to be.

In gratitude for all that you are and will be, I am your beloved, Jesus-Sananda.

Received January 17, 2019

7
The Bringers of Hope

The Divine is accessible to *all*. *Every* person can hear the pure inner counsel. You have only to be still, listen, and know *this* is real.

Dearest one, I am your beloved in whom you can trust.
In this, you can *feel* my presence in your heart.
In this, you can *feel* the comfort I bring.
In this, be at peace. For I am with you always: in quiet times, and in worrisome times.
Let my voice bring you calm. Let my help bring you assurance that all will be well.

Dearest ones, we of the Council of Light are now pervasive *on* the Earth in our communion with the multitudes.

For there is *now* in this world an upheaval of the rampant wrongs. Many are afraid of losing their control, thus they clamp down even harder.

But of this, be sure: Their time is ending and they will be no more. Their disruptive outbursts, in both words and actions, are those of children unhappy that they are losing the attention they demand. Very soon, their demands will fall upon deaf ears.

Dearest ones, you are my champions of *The Light*. For you feel *The Divine* in your bosom. You know the perfections of which I speak and, in your *inner* strength, you are now able to stand for the weak, for the damaged.

You, my dear friend, are a Bringer of Hope; and the Council of Light and I are in gratitude that you are awakened to your truth, that:

- You, in your own way, are a leader of the good that is humanity.
- You, in your own way, are a counselor to those in pain and a comfort to those who falter.
- You, in your own way, are a gift to life in this world. For you are filled with courage and you anguish not, as do the many.
- You, my friend, have taught yourself to see and to hear. Now you are sharing your learnings with all who come your way. In this way, you are a blessing in the world. And what you require will come to you.

Dearest, know this: The world is *a breathing force.* And the pain that humans have wrought *now* will be repaired, and all that is fearful will be remedied.

Dearest, this is an Era of enormous transformations—of individuals, of nations.

In this, remember, it is all for healing: of the earth, of forbidden thoughts, of harmful actions.

This—*now*—is the time.

Now the earth restores itself.

Now humanity remembers its original Intention: to live at-one with *the earth.*

Today, be at peace. Pull in the beloved crown of *Light* and surround yourself in its dimensional comfort. For when you call on *The Light* and bathe in it and seek its counsel, so it is.

We of the Council of Light are now reaching out to the multitudes. We bring strength. We bring support. We change hearts and minds.

Those who prefer destruction are facing their final days. Of this, you can be sure.

Thus, believe in the good of humanity and lift up all who suffer. That is the only test and the only life that brings peace in you.

I *am* Jesus of Nazareth. I am Sananda, *The Light of God.*

In this, be the good that you are, and all of humanity will know your compassion.

Received January 18, 2019

8
Humanity's Restoration and Awakening

Dearest humanity, we of the Council of Light now reveal to you that *we* are your ancestors. We preceded you in lives physical, most of us on Earth, in at least one incarnation.

We behold your brilliance when you open your hearts to the love of all. We reverently now show you the way to fulfill your original inheritance: that of Lightbearers. For humanity, you were each an angel, every one of you.

> Dearest ones, I am your befriender Jesus of Nazareth. In my eternal being, I am called The Beloved. My essence is *The One Who Stands with The Great Divine*. I am one of the many who have shown the way to peace.

Dearest ones, this is also *your* destiny. You were not divined out of The Void to be angry. You came into *Light* as one who sees all and values all. That is your original Self.

And *this* is your human path: To reinstill yourself with such appreciation of all life and reverence for *The Divine* from which we all came that you rise into your highest stature.

In this way, you fulfill who you really are: a Lightbearer, showing the way, that all beings on Earth may rediscover the inner *Light* and believe in their own good Nature.

Dearest ones, this world is shifting in consciousness. The peoples, in *all* the nations, are awakening into realizing that they are not in life only to serve themselves—but to be beacons of hope and insight, that they will restore their own inner *Light* and inner *knowing,* and also the *Light* of all within their reach.

Dearest ones, this day is your glory. On this day, humanity turns— away from the foment of the few who would cause all fury, *toward* a spiritual courage that bows to none but the truth of *Light* that is apparent to those who see.

Trust your inner Counsel in this. For *The Good* is now showing you the way to divest yourself of the foment of the destroyers. *The Good* is inspiring you to, forthwith, stand tall and speak clearly and deny the abusers their power. Grant them not.

For in these days of humanity's restoration and awakening to the *Light* born in all, you are kindling your strength of will and purpose. And this, my dears, is how you are given the understanding of how to stand against the mighty and to restore your own freedoms, which are yours by the grace of life.

No one has an inborn right to dominate others. When your own heart is pure and forgiving, *that* is when your strength is the strength of angels.

Let us be with you and show you the way. We are your allies, in peace and in honesty. We are your Counselors, when you heed our calls to safety and to be forewarned.

Look to your brethren with compassion, and the right path of justice will be shown to you.

We are your allies, in peace. And we align you with the angels who guide and protect all who seek balance and the way of freedom.

For every human being is born to be free and to live by *The Conscience Within* that guides you. In this, you can be assured and also rest in knowing that the outcome for *all* is a world of greater *Light*.

For you have set your sights upon justice. And this is what humanity is now birthing: a *lighter* world.

I am your beloved, Jesus-Sananda.

Received January 20, 2019

9
The Frequency That Creates Life

Dearest ones, let us all today know who we are—you and all of humanity, and also the Council of Light.

We are *all* born of The Void. We are *all* born out of the angels. We are *all* one in *The Great Consciousness* that breathed presence *into* us.

Why?

We are alive as conscious beings because *The Great Divine* let us come into existence. This *Essence* of *All That Is* breathed life into form out of *all that was not.*

Life is what we are. We are each *The Presence* in the core of our being. We are each a spark of *The Great Light* that created life out of *the what was not.*

Dearest ones, I am one of you. We are the same. We all came into presence, as form, as bequeathed from The Void. We all came into presence through the vibration called *Love*—which was and is the *fodder* that manifested *all* matter.

- Love is the fodder of our beings. Love is what *created* matter, and what *sustains* matter.
- Love is a vibratory *force* that *creates* life and generates all that we are and can be.
- So, without love, we would not be and we cannot be.
- Love is the Energy of all that is.
- Love is our heart.
- Love is the deepest truth of the universe.
- Love is what is bestowed upon us when we reveal our true calling.

So, my dearest, as we explore who we are, as beings, let us also explore the *essence* of all life: the vibratory force called "love." For it is this vibratory *frequency* that *creates* life, that generates life.

So, what is love?

- Love is the *Force* that speaks into our minds, that fills us with purpose, that teaches us humility.
- Love is *The Divine* in us.

- Love is the spark of *The All That Is and Ever Was.*
- Love is the *binding* force of all existence.

Thus, when you are filled with gratitude and an open heart, you are becoming a wellspring of *The Divine.* This, then, is the *goal* of life. This is the *purpose* of being alive.

For without love, we exist not.

In your heart, feel the bliss of *The Divine* calling to you. In this, you *are* at-one with *All That Is and Ever Was.* For, in this, you know the heart of God.

I am your beloved and I am with you always. Present in spirit, *and* in body.

Hear me, *within.*

I am Sananda, the eternal name of your teacher, Jesus.

Received January 21, 2019

10
The Eight Miracles

Good morning, my dear friends. Today, we of the Council of Light reveal a plan to fully restore the original Intention for humanity.

This is your time:

- To forgive yourself, and others.
- To be kind to all, even to those you abhor.
- To be generous of spirit, even to those who have hurt you.
- To lift up your sight to the holy promises of eternal life.

For *I* am your proof.

No one dies in the mind. No one is forever lost or abandoned. Even the weary are saved, even the disgraced, even those who have caused enormous suffering.

Dearest one, I am your beloved, known on Earth as Jesus the Beloved.

I stand before you now with this assurance:

- You shall once again be remembered for your purity and your selflessness.
- *You* are a soldier of *The Light*, on Earth, walking with the fortitude of the angel you once were.
- On Earth, you are restoring your original kinship with all of life, in all of its forms. And with gratitude, you are learning to respect those who have injured you.

My dearest, those of us who have gone before you from the world, now grace you with *The Light of Forgiveness* in your heart.

For when we forgive, the angels come to us with their goodness and bestow upon us the true miracles, which are:

- Believe in your inherent good Nature, and *you* will know peace.
- Believe in the inherent good Nature of others, and *you* will sleep peacefully and live your days with appreciation of all that is given to you.

- Believe in the creatures of the earth, the air, and the waters and *you* will see the wonders of life and know that you are one of those who is blessed.
- Believe in the will of *The Divine,* which is always what is good for every soul, and *you* will live your days in reverence and respect, which is a *still* heart.
- Believe in the open path before you that reveals your full purpose, and *you* will be asked to live that purpose, and *grace* will give it to you.
- Believe in the path of respect, and *you* will be respected.
- Believe in the words of *The Divine* that are in *your* heart and in your mind, and *you* will know who you are.
- Believe in the goodwill of all who have led you and taught you, both on the Earth and in the heavens, and *you* will revere truth.

My dearest, life is always ongoing, in this world and in the worlds hereafter.

We do not end. We are forever ourselves, conscious and aware.

You, dear ones, are now touching the grace of God, as it nurtures your thoughts, your feelings, your mind, and your soul.

Now be calm and breathe in the grace bestowed upon you.

For you are coming Home to us, now, while you are still in your body.

For we need your wisdom. You are a part of us. And this world is no longer only for the weak and sorrowed. This world is for those who live the goodness they were born to be. And *that* is you.

My dearest, *this* is your time. Live the goodness you were born to be and *that* is your new home. That is *now* Heaven on Earth, for all who embrace it.

I am your beloved, Jesus of Nazareth; Sananda, the eternal flame.

Received January 22, 2019

11
The Travelers

In the beginning of *all that is* was The Void. No life in form, only Thought. No life in matter, only Consciousness.

Then *The Great Mind* breathed life and all began.

This is the origin of all, in all dimensions. The origin first of angels, and these were the right and left hands of *The One Mind.* These were and are the Voice of *The One;* the heart, the eyes, the ears.

From the angels came the worlds and all matter.

Then some of the angels wanted to experience form. So, out of their *Light* they chose to embody onto a world of their making, into that lesser vibratory frequency.

This Pleiadian world was the origin of all humans, and the origin of all you call "E.T." For this was the first Earth, known as Perona. That world died, from the misled ones—after a Time and a Time again. Those who escaped went to Orion blue star planets first, some to the Sirius dog star worlds, others to the Andromeda Galaxy.

It was a Time and a Time again before any of these and their descendants approached the blue world (Earth) in its beginnings, as it was still in its birth and not yet populated by the living creatures on it now.

The Travelers brought their knowledge to this blue world and gave it life—as they had learned through the Times from the many Travelers before them.

And, so, life on Earth came to be.

Dearest ones, this is your origin. This is who you are. All one. All the same. From the stars. From the angels. Out of The Void, where life began—for all.

Think you not it is time to stop harboring ill-will toward those who lie and deceive? And, instead, let yourselves be valiant and speak straight, without bias but only good in your heart?

Now, humanity—*now*—is your *Second Birth.* You, and all physical beings, are *now* arising into your originally intended place in *The One Mind's* hope for you: to be leaders in *charity.*

For the only saving grace is in the heart that carries not a burden of hatred or jealousy, but instead seeks to honor all others in its path.

Dearest ones, as your Befriender, let me now ask you to open your heart to soften your words and your thoughts. Think of the lost souls as wayward children who have not yet realized that they too have the divine spark within them.

I beseech you to feel their pain and to see their anguish—underneath their bluster and their rage. See who they want to be (and someday will be). For this is your only obligation in this life.

It is time—*now*—to let go of all that has held you back, and to live in the softness of the angel you once were. Soft words. Soft thoughts.

This does not mean to ignore their actions. This means to see beneath their lack of awareness. It is true that those who cause harm must be held accountable—so that they may learn.

But for your own heart, do not turn into stone—so that you will not break during challenges.

By keeping your heart tender and compassionate: You retain thoughtfulness as well as wisdom. You grow Insight, as well as how to know *how* to heal yourself and others, and to counsel others, and to protect all in your path from harm.

A tender heart is a strength because, from it, you are able to see all for just what it is and to see far beyond what most people comprehend.

The tender heart is your protector and is the Source of all that comes to you.

I am your beloved, always, Jesus-Sananda.

Received January 23, 2019

12

Awash with Tenderness

a Meditation

In devotion, today I open to you a gift: your own magnificence as an awakened human being. In this gift, you find your higher sensitivity, innate *knowing,* and life purpose.

Today, my dearest friend, open your heart to the Bliss of *inner* awareness and trusting that is exactly what you are feeling.

Feel the Bliss that fills you with joy and, in this, gratitude.

Dearest one, the inner Bliss is your natural State. It is your inborn Character. For in this conscious higher awareness—of your soul—you are able to see all you need to know, and to discern what is your path and what is not your path.

I am your counselor on this journey. I hold your hand. I speak into your mind. I harken you to believe *and* to imagine all that you would Dream.

For my dearest, I have been where you are now. I know your hardships. I know your troubles. And now I would like to teach you how to live these experiences in *grace*. For you can.

Dearest one, you and I are not so different. We both care for our friends and family. We both learned what love is, in all of its forms. We were both thrust into situations, at a young age, that we did not then understand.

Because of our similar Earth histories, I can now help you to see and to feel the inner purity that is yours, too.

Let us now begin:

Meditation

First, quieten your heart and close your eyes.

Shut out the world around you. Slowly breathe in, then out.

Again. Then again.

Allow yourself to feel the whispers of my breath upon you and around you.

Allow yourself to feel my presence with you, and my hands upon your shoulders in comfort.

Now feel the breath of angels in the space around you, and the touch of their *Light* upon your soul . . . and how this *Light* wells up in a magnificent crescendo of splendid peace and fills you, expanding, until it completely surrounds you . . .

And you feel a slight electric tingling.

And a *knowing* fills you, and you begin to *remember:*

This is who I really am. *This* is me.

And in this bliss, you are awash with tenderness and a sweet joy. In you is only the bare goodness of all life. In you is only a pure serenity.

Linger in this serenity now . . .

Imbibe it . . . Breathe it . . . Surrender to it . . .

For this is your natural Self.

My dearest, be *still* now.

Just be.

I am your beloved, the fire of your protection, Jesus.
I am Sananda, eternal, and forever your friend.

Received January 24, 2019

13
The Council of Light

We are one. All of us.

Dearest ones, let this day be your new beginning.

Today lift up your sight to the glory of all the good being done in the world.

Today invoke all of the good of which you are capable—and for which you yearn.

This is your awakening, my friends, to your kinship with each other. This is, *now,* the only focus of your life:

- To be honest at all times.
- To trust your instincts.
- To give of your talents to all who will benefit.

We of the Council of Light revere the journey you have taken. For we, too, have made it. We ourselves knew the difficulties that you face and the burdens upon your hope. We too have been thwarted and hurt.

I say this to you now as a comfort, so that you can realize that, despite the great suffering of your many days, it is also very possible *now* to leave the pain behind you.

We of the Council of Light are writing to you today to renew your faith in the goodness that is prevailing in this world, and to show you that *you* are a *Light* of hope to many who sorrow.

Let *our* hope be your encouragement. For we and I are now imbuing *you* with the gift of life: Charity to all who suffer, to do whatever you can to lift others' burdens. In this way, you release your own worries and are able to see clearly the path before you.

It is now, dearest ones. Today is your awakening to your truest path: To live in the goodwill that inspired you and that nurtures you in your dreams.

For you are now beginning to comprehend how grand is life and how possible it is to feel the bliss of angels.

I am your befriender in all matters and in all days. I am the one called Jesus of Nazareth, the Christ who rose and lives again.

In my Father's arms, as Jesus, I am forever Sananda.

Received January 25, 2019

14
The Vibration of Life

Consciousness is our being.

Dearest ones, you are consciousness.

This is self-awareness. This is not your mind. This is *not* your brain. This is all that you are, that *we* are.

Consciousness embodies the Breath of Life *and* the vibration called love—which is the *glue* that holds all together and is how we are all a part of one another and how we are all a part of *The Whole That Is.*

Life is not the brain. That is a tool for the consciousness that lives *through* us.

Life is not the physical body. That is a tool for the vibration of life—*love*—that *manifests* our bodies (in all dimensions).

Dearest ones, our bodies and our thoughts—in all the dimensions that we exist, and *always* alive—are the tools through which we are able to interact with each other, no matter *where* we are in the Forces of Life: all dimensions, physical and after; all worlds, Earth and beyond.

Dearest ones, we are Beings manifesting forms—so that we may communicate with each other. Forms vary, including in vibratory density, but nonetheless exist.

I exist, as you exist.

I have always existed as *myself,* as you always have existed as *yourself.*

And I will always exist as *myself,* as you always will exist as *yourself.*

The only caveat is that *we continue to learn.* That is how we change. But our basic Character is who we always are.

That is not the character of our poorer habits. We are eventually the character of our interests and what motivates us. We are eternally the Character of our best Nature.

In the physical worlds, we are challenged to hone our interests and to improve our appetites, so that we learn to choose what is best for *all,* and why.

Why the best for all?

Because, yes, we literally *are* all a part of each other and a part of the whole.

In the physical, it is harder to comprehend that we are not actually separate beings. However, we can *learn* to feel the presence and thoughts—the *life force*—of any other living person, or creature.

Because, we *are* all a part of each other. We *are* all consciousness—which is the *stuff* of being.

We are all of the innate universal force that is the *glue* of all that exists. We call it *love,* because when we are reverent of life and of each other, that is what we feel. But love is actually the *force* that binds us, that binds *all.*

Dearest ones, I may no longer be in the same physical density, but I am still *me.* And this is true of everyone.

And, yes, I am still learning—how to be the most generous in my heart, how to temper my concerns, how to be open to new endeavors.

We do not ever stop learning. For all of us, from The Beginning, are curious beings.

We have always strived to be more than we are. Even I. Even you. Because growth of our consciousness—as a part of The Whole—is who we are. Who we always have been. Who we always will be.

Even I.

Even you.

And I now embrace you, my dearest ones, with all the compassion I have grown, the compassion of one being for another.

And I can tell you this: *Your* life, as it is *now,* is only the beginning.

Forever your friend, I Jesus am the *Light* of the *The Divine*—as are you.

I am eternally, Sananda.

Received January 26, 2019

15
The Star Born

Dearest ones, as we today embark upon a new Era for humanity, I can avow that you are entering a new level of understanding of your place in the universes. For at no other time has it been more clear that you, humanity, are not alone in the universe.

In *this* Era is the arrival of your forebears, in such a way that it is no longer secret and no longer hidden.

In *this* Era is the communication with those who shaped this world, in such a way that you will not be afraid and you will see that they are just as you will be in the millennia ahead.

For, my dearest ones, humanity originated *before* this Earth came to be.

Today, I and the Council of Light can avow that many of humanity's sisters and brothers from the stars already live among you.

This is why you are being awakened to knowledge of the origin of all physical beings like humans—who have been since The Beginning and even *before* the creation of all the worlds.

So, my dearest ones, be humbled that *you* are an example of what has gone before you.

Today it is time to extrapolate what this means for you and all the peoples of Earth. It means learn to embrace your fellow Earthlings, for it is soon that the knowledge of the Star Born will be evident.

And in this way, it also will be evident that humanity is *kin* to all those who existed before.

For you are like them, in appearance and in fortitude.

For humans have always explored, to understand.

And now, even on Earth, again humans are doing the same.

Exploring the heavens and the stars is an inborn yearning to know, but it is prodded by a *memory*.

And now I myself can attest, as well, that the worlds know that *you* are awakening and will be round about in due time.

This is one reason it is critical to learn to accept yourselves and to accept each other. For the only way to absorb those into your lives who are Star Born is to learn humility and gratitude. For that is the way of life in the universes for the leaders and the multitudes.

Be assured, the days are imminent.

I am your beloved, Jesus-Sananda.

Received January 27, 2019

16

The Creator

Dearest ones, in the *Light* of who you are—born an angel, out of The Void—I now invoke your *inner knowing* through a message of encouragement from our creator, *The One Mind,* of which we all are a part:

> "My dearest souls, lift up your sight to the Heavens, from whence you came. For all that you see above you is the origin worlds.
>
> "You are my blessed creations and have brought favor upon yourselves; not for your ingenuity, not even for your explorations of the stars and now your own Earth—but because you are *now* arising into the true blessing of life: a heart willing to embrace all of those you do not understand.
>
> "For a heart that is devoted to living with the inner strength called *compassion* is a mind awakening to your true purpose in life: to be at-one with all. In this way, you honor the intention of your birth into self-awareness: to see all as a part of the whole.
>
> "It is in this great arrival, *now,* of your increasing self-awareness and goodwill toward all, that you as a whole are now arising into your adept Selves: those awakened not only to the realities of your ancestors in the stars but awakening to your own path of service.
>
> "It is because of this that blessings now come to you. For this, you are supported. For this, you receive the good in life that helps you to fulfill the work you now give out.
>
> "I Am *The One Who Breathed Life,* and so it was."

Dearest ones, keep in mind that *The One Mind*—our Source of life, out of The Void—is the *Spark* of Life that brought forth all you see before you and above you; not just Earth, but all the worlds, since The Void.

We of the Council of Light have been physical, just as you are now. That is why we can understand your hardships.

But we also learned peace in the midst of strife, and that is what we bring to you now—that you may humbly let go of resentments and fears and, instead, embrace the grace that is your own purity of mind.

Grace heals you, and heals others. Let this be all that you seek to be, and all else that you need will be given to you.

I am your beloved, now and always, Jesus-Sananda.

Received January 28, 2019

17
The Path to Serenity

Good morning, lovely souls. Today we discuss the values to live by for peace in the heart.

When we are kind, all around us feels lighter, more full of sweetness and easier to navigate. This is the way of a master.

When we revere life and treasure it, we are in harmony with all the many kinds of creatures and beings. For all beings seek to live at-one, in their own kingdoms.

It is the path of serenity to live by honor. When we speak truth, we open the whole world to hear us, and this lifts us up in our hearts. For the pure of heart *are* the representatives of the angels, on Earth.

Let us, therefore, be grateful for our good fortune. For it is bestowed on us when we are flexible and generous in our dealings with others.

These are the path of a master, who is a living example of inner strength, which is never to abuse another but only to respect all else that is.

In this way, you are now walking. This is your path in this life, dearest ones. For you already embrace the desire to serve, and that is the key to Heaven and all that it can bestow.

All that you hunger for, and all that you require in your physical life, is now at your doorstep. Simply embrace the grace of your true Self, and you will be able to see, hear, and know when the door opens. It is before you.

I am your beloved, always your friend, Jesus of Nazareth, the one who is called the son of God. But my friends, *every* person is a child of God. For all of us came from *The Great Mind's* desire that we exist.

And so we are here. I am but a little further on the path.

You are walking with me. It is for this that I am grateful. We are friends in our travels throughout this life, and many others.

Always, Jesus-Sananda.

Received January 29, 2019

18
The Dominant Trait of the Majority

My dearest ones, let this day be your homage to all that you believe is good for humanity and *in* humanity. Let this be the day you praise and honor those who have graced your life *and* graced your world.

For this is a day to be happy, a day to be glad. You are, indeed, opening your inner wisdom and allowing it to blossom. So that, not only will you now find the goodwill you have sought to see and experience in this world, but now you truly will give it.

This life is your step into full awareness of your own potential, so that you may embrace it and also the fullness of every soul you see around you.

When your heart is open, you are able to see others' inner grace, and this fills your whole being with gratitude to be alive. When you allow yourself to see others' true selves—their innate goodness—you yourself are filled with such a bliss that you cannot contain it.

My dearest, this day you are awake to the *Light* of every soul and the good that is in the world, that is now also becoming the greater portion of humanity.

For here is the delightful promise fulfilled:

Humanity is cresting into its higher devotions. This is all unfolding in every heart. Even the darkest is unable to ignore the new flood of generosity and goodwill that is growing exponentially worldwide. In every corner of this Earth, now the dominant trait—of the majority—is: *"I am your brother, I am your sister. We are one, and we are in this world together."*

Dearest, this growing attitude—of the multitudes—is a crescendo of goodwill, across the face of the Earth, and in the abundance of hearts and minds.

As each soul awakens to his and her true potential, this new attitude awakens. For it is the core truth of who you all are. Who we *all* are.

This is how humanity is arising—*now*—into your original Intention. This is how you reject the voices of doom and despair. For when your own heart can see the potential—it already has been born in the multitudes . . . and already truly has begun.

This is your time, dearest one. This is humanity's time as well.

Be assured, every step you have taken has led you to *this* life and *this* moment. For you are not in this life for yourself alone, but for the whole. Your ideas and talents and voice are not for your life only—but are for the whole.

That is why you are here, dear friend. You are a beacon of joy. You bring clarity, softly.

And we of the Council of Light are here to advise and unfold the path before you, that your journey may be lovely, that your opportunities may be sweet, that your true good Self may now be free—in the world.

This day, live as one blessed. For you are. This day, you are opening yourself to be a blessing for all.

I am your beloved, Jesus-Sananda.

Received January 30, 2019

19

Humanity's Emergence

Dearest ones, I hearken you to open your eyes to the good that abounds all around you.

We of the Council of Light (ascended masters, meaning we were once third-dimension physical) are happy to report the glowing iridescent *Light* of awakening souls all over planet Earth, in every nation, *every* nation, and every spot north to south. You are truly beautiful as you shine your *Light* upward and outward, as you glow your inner joy. This is a magnificent sight.

We also gratefully welcome you—dear souls—into the circle of our experience, as we bestow on you what we have learned, not only from our many Earth lives but also from the archives called the Akashic Records. This *living* body of knowledge is always expanding. Thus, we are able to share with you the wisdoms of the past millennia as well as what is just ahead in the Earth experience.

For time is more elusive than you think. We see who humanity was—and also who humanity is becoming.

And we joyously can now report to you that the whole body of humanity has now passed the critical "point of no return."

In other words, the entire populace has *now* amassed such a wealth of goodwill as to have arisen in *the compassionate scale* to accepting others and all of life with reverence.

Yes, indeed, that is the gauge of *spiritual conscience* and the measure of one's grasp of being serene and of such a temperament as to be open to all that is unlike oneself.

It is in this changing emotional attitude that you are now able to emerge from humanity's days of cruelty as the dominant trait—to being splendidly caring and giving of yourselves that others' lives may be easier. This, my dears, is the measure of maturing into your true Nature.

So, dear ones, with gratitude for your awakening kindness, we now offer you our personal assistance and counsel at a more pure level of transmission than you before could perceive.

So listen to your heart, and listen for the whispers of insight, as you are guided further in your life's journey. For, now, the path is wider and farther for you. Angels abundantly surround you and counsel you, as do we.

All of this is so that you, *now,* may lift out of your struggles *into* the purpose *you* chose for *this* life, as your unique self.

For that, *now*—yes—Dream. And do.

For—*yes!* It is time.

It is time to take the steps toward your fulfillment. And through it all, I am with you.

I am Sananda, the *Light* called Jesus, the eternal Flame of reason and hope. And so it is.

Received January 31, 2019

20

Your True Identity

Dearest ones, on this glorious day let us give praise for all that we have. Let us be kind to all on our way. Let us be joyful for the good that flows from us. Let us be forthright, just, and fair.

These are the temperament of a soul awakened to the inner Self. These are the breath of life. These are the forces of goodwill in our lives, both toward all living beings and also toward ourselves.

In this way, dearest ones, you are restoring your favor in Heaven. In this way, you are rekindling your place in Heaven. In this way, you are recalling what it means to live with grace in your heart.

Dearest ones, let this be the day you re-invoke the inner truth of your Identity. For in these manners, you are remembering the calling of the angels to you. In these manners, you are living up to your splendid Self—which is *Light*.

Let your *Light* so shine in the world. For that is your true Identity.

You are not your challenges and struggles. You are not your moments of despair or regret.

You are the *Light* of your original Self—the birth of you as a self. And that is you forever. That is who you've always been.

Embrace and breathe in the holy *Light*. For it is already in you and all around you. And I see it in you.

I am your beloved Jesus, always Sananda.

Received February 1, 2019

21

Humanity's Group Consciousness

Dearest souls, on this bright day, we of the Council of Light hereby prepare you for the news of tomorrow. Yes, indeed, Earth is changing its level of vibration, and all on it as well.

All of humanity are undergoing a shift in awareness about who are all the peoples. In this refreshing new appreciation of the value of each person is *now* an upsurge of selfless giving. For the hearts that once were stone are now softening.

Dearest ones, this softening is a strength. It means you no longer harbor ill-will toward those who have hurt others. Instead, you now can see that they also have been stone. And even though they must be shown the error in their actions, they now will begin to become softer in their actions toward others.

It is not anyone's place to abuse or kill others. And in a lifetime yet to come, this will become clear to those who have.

Yes, such illness must be treated while they are in the world. Yes, they must be restrained. But not with hard hearts, only with clear eyes.

Dearest ones, the greater number of humanity, in all nations, are now able to face their abusers—at all levels of society—with an uprightness that demands a rightful halting to such behaviors.

In this, you are embracing your place among the honorable. For it is *just* to say *no* to any and all who proffer and spew threats and whose demeanor is to flaunt their arrogance upon others with whom they disagree.

Yes, it is a rightful action to say *no* to them and to spell out their harmful actions, that they may be thwarted from further injuring of anyone.

Thus, when we say, "turn the other cheek," that does not mean allow anyone to be ignored of their crimes, whatever their station in life. We mean, see them for who they are and place them in restraint; yet with clear eyes, not with anger.

This doesn't mean that you will not sorrow. Of course, when any person or peoples are killed or maimed, it is an open heart that cries out, "No!" When any creature or person is treated with monstrous actions, it is natural to feel their pain and to decry, "No more!"

What I and the Council of Light are saying is: You can feel the others' agony, even your own, without your own goodness being hardened. You can see to the justice they deserve—for the good of the whole—without being angry yourself, only with a clear knowing that restraint is justice.

Dearest one, I write of such matters because—yes, though the multitudes are awakening to their own good lives and they live with honor and humility—yes, there are still those who do not. And whoever they are, whatever their rank or position, each and every one of them must justly be restrained and be thwarted from further damage to any others—people, children, animals.

This is a courteous thing to do—for the many. For remember: *All* peoples are a *single* consciousness and, thus, a single body. All peoples, and *all* living forms feel the pain wrought upon any other.

This *Group Awareness* is why killing is to be stopped, maiming is to be stopped.

This Group Awareness is also why it is important—for the heart of the whole—to do so without harboring vengeance. Rectify others' cruelty without yourself doing any harm, without yourself angering in your own victimhood, without yourself being turned dark in hatred.

My friend, remember, your beauty is in your *grace,* and grace is born in *forgiveness;* not for others' hurtful actions but of the soul who has done such a hurtful thing.

Forgiveness is not to ignore or evade another's cruelty. It is seeing with clear eyes and a heart free of hatred.

When you can do that, yes the other must be restrained from any further harming of the innocents—yet your own heart is steeled with a calm, clear judgment, only for the right balance of the good of the whole.

This, my dear, is the clear, calm reason that goodness brings to you.

Do not despair. The situation of this world is now in a fierce *restoration* of what is good for the whole.

- Be your kind self, and you will know your way.
- Be your wise self, and you will know the way.
- Be your good self, and the path before you will be clear.

I am your beloved, who died and has risen. The way to peace in your heart is to abide only those whose hearts are also filled with a desire to live in honor and respect of other persons.

I am Jesus-Sananda.

Received February 2, 2019

22
How We Stop Our Inner Hauntings

Dearest ones, let us today be grateful for the good in our lives, that we will be imbued with the grace of God. Let us today be filled with an enormous joy, that we may feel the joy of the angels who are round about us.

In this, we are filled with gratitude for all that has happened in our lives. For in this way, we are able to forgive the hurts of others upon us and to know that the joy of being alive is what kindles our spirit.

In this way, we are able to see the good in others. In this way, we are filled with appreciation of all that is given to us and for us. In this way, we are able to know who we were born to be.

This is how we awaken, my dears. We let down our anger. We open our hearts. In this way, we are able to be filled with the miraculous moments of consciousness, which is to know, *"I Am."*

When we are able to embrace our original Self, the "I Am" aspect of *The Great Mind,* that is when we begin to grow in *humility*—which is the salve on all of our wounds.

- For it is humility that opens the doors to all we have sought.
- It is humility the rekindles our nature of graciousness.
- It is humility that reveals to us our true nature, a child of God.

Dearest ones, there is no secret wisdom. It is abundantly in your own heart when you begin to allow yourself not to fear.

Fear is the only thing that keeps you from growing in heightened awareness. Fear is the only thing that stops you from hearing the *Inner Counselor,* who is *always* with you. Fear is what stops you from seeing what is harmful to you.

For when we fear, we are unable to be in our own mental grace, which is peacefully, *"I Am. And all that I seek comes to me."*

Dearest ones, believe in your own *inner knowing* and it will be there. That is the grace of God in your life and, with it, silence in your heart from all that has plagued you.

As you embrace the good in your life, the hauntings stop.

> Dearest, I have been where you are. I know the hardships. I know the struggles. And I found strength through embracing the good in my life. I was whole and strong of mind. I was in favor with many devout friends. My mother comforted me. My wife lessened my concerns for the path before me.
>
> So this I know, for I have been there:
>
> Whatever your circumstances in life, whatever the abuses or hardships, you *can* be the *Light* you *are* in your soul.

You have always been this *Light,* a caring and compassionate soul. This is who you are *now*. You have only to believe, *"Yes. I Am."*

Let the *Light* of good be what gives you strength. For in acting upon your goodness, you will be filled with the love you have missed. And this is a love that heals all suffering and shows you the way to be in the world.

Always your friend, the Christed One, I am known in the Heavens as Sananda. Blessed be.

Received February 4, 2019

23

How Jesus Came to Be in the World

Dearest ones, let us today journey in our memories to *The Origin* of all that is.

When we first came into consciousness as fully formed Beings of Light, we were in awe of the splendor all around us. For we were imbued with the powers of creation and we—as angels—created the dimensions of all existence. In these dimensions came, then, forms of the life we had envisioned.

We are the believers who lived out of *The Breath* that brought us out of The Void into the most extraordinary existence—as Beings of Light. We were filled with joy and the ecstasy of awe. We were abundant, with endless days of pure perfection in everything we, too, then created.

For the Creator is not a person, but is an *Awareness*. And out of this womb, we and all *Light* came to be.

Endowed with the Creator's gifts, we also breathed life into beings, giving them *our* qualities of curiosity and appreciation.

Dearest ones, you and I all began as the angels of all the Heavens. When we chose to become physical, we were seeking to learn more, to feel the levels of our being.

You—as did I—chose the Earth world not out of a desire to control or suppress, but to give our presence and wisdom to the humans already in the world that they may be healed of their forgetfulness. For they were sorely lost in their anguish.

> This is how I also came into the world, as Jesus. Although I experienced many lives in the physical—as you also have—in the life as the Teaching Angel *called* Jesus, I knew a greater awareness than ever before.
>
> I remembered the Heavens. I recalled the lives of all I had been. I studied the Ancients. I learned to *breathe in* the power of life. And I regained the sweetness of the original Good I had been.
>
> In my full being, then, I was able to restore not only the bodies of those I passed by, but also to tender their hearts to remembering the Good they were.

> This is how the miracles became known.
>
> As word spread, it was a fury of curiosity. For every person wants to be saved from sorrow.
>
> This is the reminder I brought to give to all peoples: That *every* person is already ordained to live in a blessed world.

You, my dearest, already have been saved, in your own *conscience*. All I did was to awaken the hearts of men, women, and children to their original Selves.

Every person is already ordained in the universal Good. You already have the whole of creation in you. You already have the gifts of Insight.

In this, you are whole. In this, you are able to know what is real. In this, you are able to take your dream to its fullest expression.

Dearest ones, you were created out of The Void. You have always been the fulfilled expression of the Creator.

You—like me—have always held the powers of love inside you. And that is the blessing you *now* bring to the world. For your wisdom is needed.

My dearest ones, your life is to live with *gratitude* and to bless the life of every being around you.

Bless them by living in your own best Nature, the Being of Light who came into life to serve the *All That Ever Will Be.*

You are in this life to be a teacher of goodwill. With your heart open, every word you speak is with tenderness. That is what every heart yearns for, again.

In humility, I am your brother, Jesus, eternally Sananda.

Received February 6, 2019

24
The Spark of a True Human

Dearest ones, this is a day to be glad. For the world as you have known it is dynamically changing, structurally and politically.

This is from an upward expansion of peoples' hearts and minds, in *all* nations. This is from the peoples no longer succumbing to intimidation and threat.

The world around, humanity is taking hold of its own needs and denying the pursuers who are cruel. Humanity is—*now*—arising into its intention to live for the whole, and is tremendously rejecting the hostilities of the domineering leaders. Humanity is—*now*—surging in a new threshold of embracing rightness as a code of life, and dispelling—with outrage—all in power who seek nothing but more gain in their own pockets.

Dearest ones, although greed and murder have ruled the Earth since its beginning: *This now halts.*

For today, the shift in self-awareness is the birth of a new peoples, those who respect the whole and refuse any longer to be subject to any others' inequitable demands.

Such new self-awareness is the *spark* of a true human, one who embraces generosity and kindness. For that is the *Light* carried within.

Those people—the few—who demand your fortunes for themselves are facing dire consequences. Whereas, those whose hearts are pure are facing blessings abundant. This is all *now* transpiring.

In this century and the next millennium, humanity is earning its *Light* crowns. For though there is strife, and cruelty will be in disdain, those who hold the coffers do not give in willingly.

You, dearest ones, are now surprising yourselves at your strong resistance to others' efforts to overpower you. Yet this is right.

No other persons have the right to dictate how you must live. Only your own mind has that right. And when you are awakened in your awareness to the greater truths of life, it is your talents that shed *Light* and offer refuge. For your talents are your own God-given gifts to humanity.

Dearest ones, therefore, today rejoice. For you are awakened to your heart's call. And the angels stand with you, in abundance, as your counsel and as your guides.

In this way, you are able to find and live the holy dream of your soul, which is to share your own experiences that others also may discover that power is in a heart that knows itself.

I am your beloved, Jesus-Sananda.

Received February 7, 2019

25

The Wayshowers and The Peacemakers

Dearest ones, we of the Council of Light imbue you with the knowledge of all the Ages. We are imbuing into your physical memory all that has ever been and all that is now unfolding. We are imbuing you with the powers of understanding and a willingness to learn what has, before, been only partially revealed.

Today, my dearest ones, we the angels of all the Heavens, we the souls who have gone beyond Earth, we the ones who oversee humanity—today we imbue into your consciousness what has been called the Mysteries.

Of this I can avow—I Jesus of Nazareth, now eternally a Being of Light—that all you have sought to see and hear and know is accessible to you.

And now we the thrones of Heaven bring to you what we have been given to show you—from the ancient Source of all life, from the *Mind of All That Is,* from the Source of all experience and all that is to come. We now reveal to you how you may be aware of the Greater Reality and *bring* it *into* your full waking state.

For now *is* the time. Now *is* the time to be fully present.

Dearest ones, this book is one of thousands being imbued into the minds of humanity, today. This book is our Voice sharing with you not only what has been but what is now *in* becoming.

This book is our gift to you, from the authority of the Most High, so that you will be even more sure and more glad of your place in the world, at *this* time.

Dearest ones, you whose hearts seek to bring peace to others—*you* are the Wayshowers on Earth, among the multitudes who *do* feel the call to their fullest Selves.

Dearest ones, you have not heard or seen these messages by chance. You come to them through the call of your spirit—that *you* may be more fully conscious, in *all* that you do: in your busy, arduous physical life.

For you have asked, and I now answer:

- Be a voice of God, in your choices and in your daily work.
- Be a voice of God as you open the door and go out into the world each day. Not for your own glory—but as a voice of peace.

Dearest ones, in your world there is a great shift, and now you can be a peacemaker—not only by your words but by your actions. It is not enough to think, *I want to help*. It is time to do it.

Listen to the inner truth that shows you the way. For you do already know your talents. Believe in who you are.

That talent is your voice to the world.

That talent is how you show the inner peace, as you discover it.

That talent is how you are a peacemaker.

For your talents are your fullest Self speaking *through* you, to lighten the world. And whoever you are, this is *your* way to add to the illumination that is *now* shining in and through the hearts of *all* humanity.

Dearest ones, live your fullest Self and you are activating your true calling. Whatever your talents, these are *your* voice to the world—as a peacemaker.

Beloved, you are inspired. Trust that which lifts you up into your own fullest heart. For that is you. And we are at your side.

More will be shared. But today, know this:

You are a wayshower, living your truth, and *that* is your *Light*.

I have come before to *you,* as to others. Now hear me:

I am your brother. I am he who guides you. I am the eternal Self of the one who lived as Jesus of Nazareth.

And I am now come again. I am eternally Sananda.

Received February 8, 2019

26
The Full Immersion

a Meditation

Dearest ones, here we are together, in our goodwill. This is a blessed time to be alive. This is a time to be joyous that you are on the Earth, *now*.

For *now* humanity is rising into your original Intention. *Now* you are coming into the fullness for which you were created, out of The Void.

Dearest ones:

- On this day be sure, humanity will not forever be in the shallows of reason.
- On this day be sure, you also are now coming into your fullest voice of expression as a being born in *Light*.

We of the Council of Light bring to you the awareness you have sought of your original Self.

You are our kin. You and we are the same. We are no more than you in our hopes for humanity. What we do bring is the full vision of what you are now coming to see.

In this Era, you surpass your angers toward all who are unlike you. In this Era, you arise into the grace of consciousness, from which you can see all that is. In this Era, you *all* are immersed in the blessings of Heaven. For in this Era, all that you seek—when for the good of all—is given to you.

Dearest ones, I am only an instrument to reveal to you your innate Good Nature. I am only one of many showering your hearts today with the teachings of the Ages. We are coming to you now, in great abundance, that you may know who you were created to be—each and every one of you.

We of the Council of Light and the multitudes of the angels bring to you now the serenity you have sought. For it is real. It is tangible. And it is yours.

Let us now open the Gate for you to this unfolding new world. Let us now show you the way into your own serenity. And how this is the mainstay not only in your mind but also in the physical daily challenges that assault the good heart.

Meditation

Dearest ones—

Now, be still.
Slow your breath.
Slow your thoughts.
Feel the gentle *Light* flowing into you.
Feel its warmth softly bathing you.

Now allow yourself to drift in this inner quiet.
Just be with it.
No place to be.
In this moment, only in the inner quiet.

Let it flow in you and through you,
as you are flowing with it in your breaths.
Letting the gentle flow lull you as a child.
Letting the gentle sweetness hold you as a child.
Being at peace, in the moment.
The graceful *Light* in you.

Dearest one, you already are this gentle *Light*. In your being, in your original Self, this is who you already are. You are only remembering.

Allow this now to breathe *into* you with every breath.
Gently.

Be at peace, dear soul. This is your time. You are now in the full immersion of your true Nature. In harmony, without a need to prove yourself.

Your only goal: To live in serenity and to serve all who need you. Just by being who you always have felt you are and have sought to be.

Be this now.

I am your beloved, Jesus-Sananda.

Received February 9, 2019

27
The Quieting Breath

a Meditation

My dearest friends, today the Council of Light and I share a story.

In The Beginning there was nothing—except a *Mind* that saw all. This *Mind* was able to perceive a great experiment: humanity.

When humans first came to be, we were but ideas in *The Mind*. Yet out of that Nothingness first came the angels, whose form is higher dimensional *Light*.

It is from the angels that all the worlds came to be. It is from the angels that all physical humans and sentient beings were born.

This, my friends, this is how you and I and all the Masters of Wisdom came to be, in Time.

The Origin is a physical manifestation of the Original Nothingness. — For all was but a Void. Yet in that there existed a Consciousness—which is the *fabric* of all that exists, ever was, and ever will be.

We of the Council of Light share this story not to disavow science. For science is the recognition of *how* consciousness exists *and* runs everything.

In this story, we are seeking to expand the reach of Thought and Imagination. For the comprehension has only just begun.

As science reaches further, it will become more clear that all that seems physical is but one dimension, and there are so many levels of existence that the human mind cannot see them or even imagine them.

But for you.

Dear friends, you who awaken to your spiritual bond with the angels are activating not only your mind—but your eternal consciousness.

This is how you are able to hear the voice of all the Masters of Wisdom and the angels, and even the Travelers, both off and on the planet.

It is through your activated higher consciousness that your higher abilities are awakened, giving you the keen sense of *knowing* what is otherwise not evident.

Your higher consciousness (already in you) is only a breath away. Literally.

My dearest friends, accessing your full knowledge and how to see and hear beyond the physical mind is, quite simply, through regularly practiced *breath*.

The one tool that raises your vibration into your full awareness is *breath*.

Therefore, I will be sharing some techniques on this that I have learned. Because it is easy. It is simple. It is how you *still* your active mind and *quiet* your thoughts—so that, then, you are able to hear the subtle inner *whispers* coming *to* you from the Beings who live all around you, all conscious yet in higher dimensions.

This is the most important tool for accessing your own higher consciousness.

Meditation

Breathe, my dear. Breathe.
Softly, gently, steadily.
Slowly, quietly, evenly.
Breathe in . . . slowly.
And let it out . . . slowly.
No rush.
Just be.

Just be with this calming rhythm.
Just let the breath flow *through* you.
In . . .
And out . . .
And in again . . .

Letting everything go.
Letting go of all else.
All that matters in this moment is *the quieting breath.*
And you are becoming *still.*
And the breath is releasing *all* that you carry.
The breath is releasing all that holds onto you.
And there is nothing else.

There is nothing else but this even, steady *quieting breath.*
Breathing . . . slowly . . . steadily.
Quieting your body.
Becoming *still.*
Letting all go.
Letting all go.
Only in the quieting breath.

. . . . . .
. . . . . .
. . . . . .

And now, dearest one, remain in your quiet place.
This is where you have always been.
Remain in your quiet place.
. . . . . .
. . . . . .
. . . . . .

With love for all.
Feeling the blissful you . . . with every gentle breath.

And in the peace.
. . . in the peace.
. . . in the peace.

I am your beloved, Jesus-Sananda.

Received February 10, 2019

28
The Shifting Dynamic

Dearest ones, what is happening in the world? All seems to be going awry. Yes, there is much news about terror and cruelty. There is also, less reported, an abundance of human compassion.

All ages, the young to the elderly, are—*now*—more caring than at any other time in Earth's history.

Since humans began on Earth, there has been hardship and, from that, fear. As a result, people took matters into their own hands, seeking domination over others whom they saw as inferior—out of a fear that they themselves were vulnerable. This premise has controlled peoples' ideologies for many hundreds of *millions* of years. However, *now,* the tide is turning.

Although a few people in Earth's past have sought to live justly, the multitudes—being downtrodden—mostly were always in a desperate struggle for survival.

Yet—*now*—that entire dynamic is shifting.

Today, the multitudes are realizing their power—to change their own lives. And *this* awakening is an Age of enlightenment unlike any ever seen before on Earth, an enlightenment not merely of technology and science . . . but of the heart.

This new Age of enlightenment is the innate comprehension that *every* person is worthy.

This new Age of enlightenment is a deep acceptance and clarity—in the hearts of *every* man, woman, and child: that *every* life is worthy.

This new Age of enlightenment—*now* arising in the hopes and courage of *every* person on Earth—is a deep understanding that no one should suffer, that no one should be hurt or killed, that no one person should have to live in illness or pain.

Thus, arising—*now*—is a new, global belief in the value of *every* life and the right of *every* person to live with peace in the heart and mind.

My dearest ones, it is true that *these are the days long foretold.* That wars and rumors of wars are pervasive. That souls suffer grievously.

It is also true that the multitudes are now arising, to say, "No more!" and are demanding to be respected.

It is also true that millions are aware of their inner divinity *and* they live to help others.

It is also true that the very few who have only lived to exploit others are now facing an onslaught of criticism—*and* will be facing the harsh consequences of their feckless choices.

For in this *new* world—*now* arising—the good *will* prevail.

Take heart, my dear friends. I come to tell you: The time is *now*.

Good is the new rule of the day. Live by your heart's guidance and you will know the path of your own nature to, in some way, be a help, a benefit, in whatever ways your heart reveals to you, day by day.

I come to you as your friend. I am always with you as a counselor. I come to you to remind you:

You, my friend, are a *Light* in the world. Be the *Light* you were born to be. For the world needs you.

In this way, *your* own life challenges are easier to bear. Because a pure heart is filled with peace.

I love you, always. I am Sananda. He who is the *Light* of the world—

As are you.

Your beloved, Jesus.

Received February 11, 2019

29
The Great Illumination

Dearest souls, how grand is this day for humanity. The Council of Light and I see the brilliance of your opening hearts and how generous you are toward your fellow Earthlings.

This is most obvious in the nations where there has been perpetual darkness. For even the least of these, who has little, bears a helpful attitude toward his and her friends, family, and outsiders.

It is in the poorest of the world that there is a new spark of hope that life can be better. And it is these hardened souls, by way of life's hardships, who are arising in tremendous numbers to help their countrymen, especially the children.

It is in these most impoverished lands that the people are arising most remarkably, with strong wills and indomitable spirits, to care for the earthly needs of their poverty-stricken families.

It is in these lands and communities, where they have suffered the most egregious of crimes against them, that the few are becoming the many and are standing up against their domineering slaveholders and are saying, "No! No more!"

Dearest ones, peoples all across the world are finding their spirit of hope—and resilience—to defy all that has wronged them and to believe in their rights to be free. Free of control. Free of slavery. Free of poverty.

It is these now growing numbers, who have faced poverty and control for generations, who are now the brightest *Lights* on Earth—because *their* voices are piercing the shrouds that have bound them.

Dearest souls, *every* person in this world is *now* being illuminated from within, to rise up against their oppressors. It is these who have the least in the world that are the brightest *Lights*. For they feel the truth in their depths that *they* were born to be free.

This is not a new awakening of such fearsome troubles. But this is a wave of the greatest proportions ever seen. Not only a single land or people—but in *all* corners of the world. From the north to the south and every horizon, those who have been downtrodden—for generations—are *now*, as if illumined by the angels, arising as a mass and saying, "I matter! My voice *will* be heard!"

These, dear ones, are the voices speaking out who will rock the world. For in this—*now*—a Great Illumination across all boundaries is shaking the very foundations that have imprisoned minds, bodies, and souls.

And now that striking resistance to the past is arising, en masse, in all areas on this Earth—with strong wills and strong minds, saying, "We matter! We will no longer sit at the feet of the mighty! We will no longer lower ourselves to your obeisance! It is now *our* time! We are now taking what is rightfully ours, our own place at the table!"

Dearest ones, those who have been tortured and starved, for generations, those who have been killed and maimed for the joy of their oppressors—are *now* arising, in *every* land on the Earth.

And those who have stepped on them and shackled them—in mind as well as body—are now feeling the fierce resistance.

In this, The Great Illumination is shattering false ideologies and is birthing the strength of angels in the bosoms of those (in all lands) who have been brushed aside.

For The Great Illumination is not only for those who already have open eyes and open hearts. It is not only for those who hear *The Divine* speak. It is for *all* on the Earth.

Every person is being awakened. And for those whose lives and bodies have not been their own, they too are feeling the sharp awakening of the inborn power within them: "I, too!"

This, my friends, is the harsh truth of humanity's history. And now the time is here: For in The Great Illumination, all corners of darkness are brought into *The Light*. And, in that, the arrival of the newly free.

It is time, my friends. It is time that every soul on Earth know that she and he was born in liberty and shall find liberty—in *this* life.

This is the new Era, dear friends: An awakening of greater compassion, an awakening *empowerment* that is born when one is touched by the *Light* of the angel she or he once was. For *every* person is *The Light*.

And now, in The Great Illumination, *The Light* is expanding . . . and is spreading . . . and sparking to life . . . in *every* corner of the Earth.

I am your beloved, Jesus-Sananda.

Received February 12, 2019

30

Dawn of the New Earth

Hello, dearest ones. On this day, humanity is being awakened to the inner divinity that is in *every* soul.

On this day, the men, women and children of God are being awakened to the inner purity of their original Selves. And, in this, the spark of remembering is reducing the dread that has carried them forever. — Until now.

Now, my friends, the new dawn of hope is born.

On this day, my friends, you can embrace the peace that opens within you. For you are, indeed, being reborn—into the original Self you were and always have been.

Dearest friends, today is the new dawn of hope. For it is as clear as the morning sun.

Your *Lights* are brilliant in hope.

Your minds are now being illumined with clarity.

This, my friends, is the arrival of the higher wisdom within you. And in this shower of higher knowledge, you are realizing that drudgery is of the old earth and that, in the now awakening *new* Earth, humanity sees and feels the joy of life.

In this *new* Earth, you are feeling the higher calling to live purely. You are feeling the deeply personal connection with your full Identity, which is the holy original Self, as an angel.

And as this newly born self, remembering your purpose—to live in the higher purpose, to serve all—you are feeling the dawn of hope . . . and *this* is your food. This is *now* your sustenance. This is *now* the only *Light* that guides you and motivates you.

Dearest friends, *you* are in this world *as* a bringer of *Light. You* are in this world as a bringer of hope.

Hope is tangible. Hope is the food that lifts one up out of despair. Hope is the kindest gift to the world. For in the old world, sorrow reigned. But in the *new* Earth, *hope* is the *Light* that calls to every heart.

And *you* are here, *now*—in this *new* Earth—to bring hope. That is all there is.

I am your beloved, always, Jesus-Sananda. *Received February 13, 2019*

31
The Fifth Consciousness

Beautiful souls, this is a glorious day. For I and the Council of Light can attest that you are, indeed, upleveling — *right now* — into the fourth-dimension physical. *This* is the new Earth.

We are honored to watch the expansion of humanity's consciousness. You are moving swiftly now.

In this new illumination of your hearts and minds, you are becoming what you were born to be: teachers and healers of peoples' traumas.

You, my dearest, are pronounced in your personal illumination as *you* are awakening with a fullness of goodwill. And *this,* my dearest, is your personal *transcension* into the *fifth* consciousness.

For not only are you a loving person in your own family, whatever the circumstances, you are inviting the angels, for the good of all.

The *fifth* consciousness is being attuned to the well-being of the whole and teaching others how to be a part of the whole.

The *fifth* consciousness, or fifth-dimension consciousness, is caring for the group of humanity. Wanting to heal. Wanting to support.[3]

You, my dearest, have personally embraced the highest potential of your earthly body. And that is to realize, and incorporate, that you do not live for yourself alone.

You, now, have come into a full commitment to be of service to others. To reach beyond your own needs, to lift others up and to help them with your own gifts and talents.

Dearest, this is *your* birth into being a *new* human. *You* are the perfect example of what it means to become a member of *the new humanity.*

And of this, I can attest:

---

[3] These levels of consciousness are discussed in *Your Awakening Attitude of Service: In Jesus' Words, Today – on The Fifth Level of Consciousness,* which is the sequel to this First Edition.

- *You* came into this life to be a presence of counsel and tenderness.
- *You* came into this life to help others discover their inner wisdom.
- *You* came into this life to be a voice of good and of hope.

That is your purpose, my dear. And, now, you are not only invoking the understanding. You are embracing the fact that you are, indeed, ready.

Dearest, it is *your* time. Be your full Self, *now*. And *this* is your full and glad heart.

In this, you are blessed a thousand-fold. In this, you are given all you need. Because, now, you are living to help others. And *that* is the purpose of being human.

I am your beloved, always, Jesus-Sananda.

Received February 14, 2019

32
Your Full Release

Dearest ones, I and the Council of Light are incredibly happy for you, because though you may not yet have fully embraced the inner peace—it *is* growing in you.

We see it. We feel it. We see and feel the presence you are, as once an angel and now remembering the grace that is your strength.

Dearest ones, this life is the most perfect of all that have been before and, although you struggle grievously and have difficulties that are overwhelming, let me now assure you that *I* see the perfection of your soul, and *I* feel the enormous gratitude you have for life itself.

Dearest, although you have been hurt and have suffered intolerable abuses, nevertheless, in your heart you *do* know your strength—which is compassion.

Compassion toward all who have hurt you is what gives you an inner peace that no one can take away.

For when you are able to rise above the anger and rage toward others who abuse and maim, it is *you* who is rewarded with an *inner stillness*. And *that* is the rock upon which you are able to stand, even in a world that seems adrift with madness.

Of this I can assure you: Today is but a drop in your life—but it can be the *single* drop that moves the tide of your life's events, toward the better.

Think of your tears and sorrows as but drops in your lifetime. Think of your lifetime as an ocean that covers the earth. Think of the *single* drop today of sadness or regret. Now think of *that* drop as the last . . . which will unburden you.

For, today, let this be the last need to unburden your deep anguish and, instead, turn your *entire* attention *upward* to your *Light*.

Let this *Light* fill you and *bathe* you with angelic sweetness and song.

Let this *Light* so guide you through yourself, *upward* into your own tremendous heart filled with joy for what, now, you can be. For what, now, you will do.

So that, from this day forward:

- Let the *Light* be *all* that fills your thoughts and your hours.
- Let the *Light* be all that fills your needs and your sharings.
- Let the *Light* be all that you need.

And in this, from this day forward, in the *Light* as your only reason for being—expressed in *all* that you do—if there are any more tears, they are only droplets of *full release* . . . into absolute joy *and* the full realization that, at last, you understand.

This is what your life can be, always.

Dearest, I am here for you. Call on me. I will always answer.

I am your beloved, Jesus-Sananda.

The *Light* of *The Divine* is in *you*.

Received February 15, 2019

33
The Era of Good Hope

Dearest ones, let this be the day you allow yourself to feel hope for all you have dreamed. For it is *now* coming to you.

This is an Era of good hope for humanity. Though wars and disasters still seem to prevail, these will not be forever.

You can see—even now—a *Light* arising in the masses. That *Light* is their realization that all they hope for is the betterment of their loved ones.

The good in people is not for themselves. They are filled with a desire to help others. And though it is not apparent, this is—*now*—the vast majority of humanity.

Dearest ones, live your own *Light,* through an open heart willing to give, and you will be helping to reshape the world toward its intended purpose.

You are, indeed, thus a part of creating Heaven on Earth. For the many, not for the few.

A generous spirit is who you are. Let this be your *Light* and your purpose. Whoever you are, whatever your circumstances, *you* are in this life to lift up those around you. *This* is why you are in the world.

My dear, all that is transforming is for the betterment of all—and *that* is a life worth living.

I am here for you, in spirit and in body. Call on me for counsel. Your beloved, Jesus-Sananda.

Received February 16, 2019

34

Hope Among Upheavals

Dearest ones, we of the Council of Light are round about you, *now.*

Feel our presence in your heart, as the inspiration that guides you.

Let us kindle your aspirations, which will lead you up the path of greatest service.

Let us be the voice in your thoughts to give you direction and help you, always, to know which choice is the helpful one for you.

Dearest ones, you are our kin, and we embrace you for all that you are doing to help those who suffer greatly.

Let us encourage your dreams and reveal the path forward as you embark on a new more widely visible journey. For in the work you now embrace, the Heavens are with you and the thrones of angels are with you.

Dearest ones, this Earth is now in a major upheaval politically, which affects the lives of all who live now.

It is, therefore, *your* purpose to bring hope and assurance that these things are the changes needed to heal the wrongful attitudes that have damaged so many for so long.

Your place in this is merely to speak with an open heart. For in this, *I* am with you, for all that you are as my vehicle to the world . . . as the power of God.

Thank you for being our helper in this time, to bring a new way of seeing and hearing. For in this, we of *The Light* can bring renewed faith in the peoples whose lives are touched and enhanced by the words given through you.

Dearest ones, this is *your* time to simply say, *"Yes, I will do this."* And know that *I* am with you.

No other is as you, in the way that you feel my presence and hear my hopes *through* you.

So you can know that all *I* say is for the good of all. And all that I am sharing with you is to illuminate how the world perceives me.

Let us now invoke the presence of the angels. For they, too, are your counsel and your protection. Wherever you go, we are there. We are round about you. And as you walk in *Light,* our counsel is round about you.

This is the Lord. Your friend. Your benefactor. And *this* is my service to you.

The path that is opening I have set before you.

It is *my* voice they hear. It is to my request that they have called.

And now the path is wider and brighter—because *now* the need is great.

And with your help, all the world will feel my presence, as I am now born anew and these are *my* words to the many.

I am Jesus of Nazareth. I died and rose again.

And now, my dear friends, I am returned. In your heart. *Through* you.

Received February 17, 2019

35
The First Insight of Awakening

Dear ones, let us today understand what is going on in the world, as I know much is hard and also is scary.

We of the Council of Light have been in physical bodies, most of us on Earth, so we do understand how terrifying life can be.

We are here now helping more people to realize that life is perpetual.

Who you are, as a self—your dreams, your emotions, your temperament—does not end. Ever.

Therefore, life is a grand opportunity to test your mettle and to shape and improve how you think and feel.

And the more refined you are in your observations, intuition, and expectations—the easier life is for you.

So, look at the world not only as one of terror, where abuse is rampant. — But as a way to utilize and grow your inborn abilities to evaluate and discern which *choices* will teach you to improve your outlook on life, and which will delay your service to others.

Life is not separate from you. The more you impart your awareness to others, the more you also grow.

So that, while the world is—still—largely in disarray, the question is, *How can you improve on that?*

For the power of creation is *yours. Your* heart and *your* imagination are the tools of creativity that can expand your life.

So, the experiences in life are merely ways to learn to open your heart and eyes. Then to build on that as you become more aware of the meaning of life and how *you* are here to make it better.

Yes, dear ones, you are here for a reason. And coming to that knowledge—at your core—is the first Insight of one who is awakening to the gifts that are *already* within you.

So, dear ones, be forever sure: The challenges of life are *not* your enemy. They are the power within that is *honing* you to your own full beingness.

It is this, that I am returned to teach. It is this—and only this—that matters.

For the experiences of life are merely your opportunities to become the full Self you once were, as an angel—and *now* even more.

For the physical challenges are the instruments of becoming fully Graced Beings, and the angels are your guides.

You, my dears, are *already* on this journey. And you are now remembering and embracing—that you may carry forth your *Light*—as a Light Beacon—throughout the world.

And always, I and the Council of Light and all the angels of Heaven watch your way and are as near to you as your own breath.

Be calm, dear ones. And be sure. The time *is* now.

I am your beloved, Jesus-Sananda.

Received February 18, 2019

36
The River of Life

Dearest ones, now it has begun. All of humanity are now being awakened—in their hearts—to the purpose of their existence: That *every* person is here to become your fullest best self and, through that, a *contributor* to others, for the fulfillment of *all.*

Life is an opportunity to discover who you were born to be . . . *and* be it.

Life is an opportunity to find the joy in your imagination . . . *and* share it.

For in this is your own true joy *and* peace of mind. For in this, you realize that the purpose of life is to feel *wondrous.*

Dearest ones, let today be your awakening to your true kindness and to your personal happiness—through developing your *inborn* talents—to their fullest—and living your talents *every* day:

- So that you are *unbridled* creatively.
- So that your heart is full with the creative flow.
- So that *you* are like a river pouring out its life force, to nourish *all* who come its way.

Dearest ones, your mind, your imagination, and your dreams for this life—*these* are the life force in you seeking to break through into *The Light.*

And when you nurture your ideas and the creative flow in you, it pours forth, as a river gives abundantly to *all* who seek its power and its sustenance.

Dearest ones, the world's problems are lessened when *you* unleash the imagination *in* you that is able to reach to *The Light.*

The world's problems are solved and healed as *you* unfold your mind's capacity and awaken the *inner* curiosity, and reveal the pure creative force that is in you: Letting it rise into *Light* with its full potential, no longer restraining your talents from the world. Instead, breathing into them the abundant *Light* of the *inborn* divinity that your soul *in* you imbues everything you do.

Dearest ones, lift up your sight to *The Light* and *feel* its life force *in* you, stirring you to magnify *all* that you are able to be in this world. Not for yourself alone—but for the whole.

For humanity is *one* body and *one* mind and, as you grow and express the highest and best that you are, so *you* become a power of *healing* in the world.

Through *your* ideas, through your words, through your voice—*you* touch every heart.

In this way, you are helping to restore humanity's Identity as Intended by The Divine Ones.

In this way, you are helping to heal people's sorrow and discouragement, and to instill hope and a fierce will, not only to survive but to be the best that *each* can be.

For the drive to grow and learn is *innate* in all of us. We all learn to rise above the weaknesses of life and to lift up into our potential Selves—which is *why* we chose physical life in the first place.

Dear one, this is *your* time. There is no time to wait. The time is *now*.
You *are* ready. And the world needs you.

I am your beloved, Jesus of Nazareth. Forever eternal, Sananda.

Received February 19, 2019

37

The World's New Innovative Thinkers

Dearest ones, let us today be prepared for a powerful new possible Earth. For this is, *now,* the beginning of a world and planet transformed.

Life as you have known it is in the early stages of a complete rejuvenation.

Do not assume this. Nor deny.

Do not fear this. Nor ignore it.

Instead, realize, it does not happen by chance.

It is from the inspired ideas of thinkers and innovators and those who are brave.

For it is the people with open minds and great imaginations who are able to envision *and* construct the remedies for building and healing the world—all societies and the planet: the earth, the seas, and the air.

This is not a small feat. Yet it can be done. And we of the Council of Light are very encouraged by the spirited ideas and solutions, worldwide.

The newer generations have grand proposals. Grand, yes, but *also* plausible.

You see, understanding possibilities requires being able to *foresee* remedies that, before, were not even contemplated.

It is these innovative thinkers who are now crafting the world's and the planet's restoration. This does require bold leadership and courageous stances, in the public eye. It *also* requires persistence.

Such improvements in the attitudes of politics are not easily embraced. Yet this is *exactly* what is required for the necessary changes. For life must *now* be renewed—at *all* levels—for the full Intention of this world to be *now* divined.

So, dear ones, I and the Council of Light ask this:

- Will *you* be a part of the earth's healing?
- Will *you* be a part of restoring a global kinship, nation to nation?
- Will *you* be a part of creating a political landscape that attends to the whole?

For these are the steps needed. Not only by a few, but by many.

And my dear friends, *every* voice is needed. *Your* voice, your perspective, is needed.

This, I your friend and befriender, ask of you:

- Will *you* now be one who speaks up?
- Will *you* now be one who leads?
- Will *you* now be one who comes into *The Light* and shines your perspective?

For that is what is needed: For this earth. For this world.

I am with you, in all that you say and do.
I am with you, in spirit and in body.
I am the voice in your heart that guides you.
Let me be your ally.
With love, I am always, Sananda.

Received February 20, 2019

38

The Age of Awakening

Dearest ones, we of the Council of Light are here for you at this time because of your opening hearts.

For it is hearts expanding in kindness and compassion that illuminate the world around you.

It is your hearts sheltering the poor that is lighting the world with hope.

It is your hearts trusting the spirit in you that is showing the world what love is.

This is why, dear friends, we are joyous to see your gratitude for all that you have.

This is why we are enormously happy to see your appreciation of the animals and the earth.

This is why we are here to help you in your own life as you seek to help the poor and the suffering. For that *is* the way of the angels.

In your awakening heart to unbridled love, you are becoming the kindred soul of the Ancients who brought you here.

In your opening to the splendors of yourself as a Light Being, you are able to see and hear the Ancients who created you.

In your willingness to feel the grace of God in your own life, you are able to understand the wisdom being shown to you.

These, my dearest friends, are the last days of a world in torment. These are the last days of rampant cruelty. For the good of humanity are arising and saying, "No. No more."

Yes, these days are many lifetimes.

Yes, these days are millennia.

Nevertheless, you have begun.

My dearest friends, keep your hearts open and your minds free.

For it is in your *new* sight and understanding that the Intention for humanity becomes known to you.

It is in your new vision and ability to hear and perceive the higher realms that you are able to know what is in your path right now. And that is: The awakening of the whole body of humanity.

For now *is* the Age of awakening—to your Intended nature: Whole, in body and in mind. Whole, in spirit and in service.

Dearest friend, we of the Council of Light and all the angels of the Heavens speak into your heart not only to guide you, not only to counsel you—but to show you that you *already* are one of us.

You, dearest, are *one* of us. Remembering.

I am your beloved, Jesus of Nazareth, the *Light* of the world. Eternally, Sananda.

Received February 21, 2019

39

Jesus Is Now in the World

Hallelujah! Praise the Lord. The Lord has come.

Dearest friends, I am returned.

In your heart, I reach across the dimensions of life to speak to you, to guide you, to show you the way.

And in the world, as a man, I am also one of you. In the flesh. And I am *now.*

Yes, my dear friends. In your lives. Seeing the hunger. Seeing the fear. Seeing the debacles.

Also seeing the rising hope and the courage of all humanity, that is: Now rising up. Now becoming one.

My dearest friends, I am a voice of conscience. I am a voice of encouragement. I am a voice of direction.

Dearest friends:

- Let not hunger prevail. *Feed the poor.*
- Let not disputes admonish. *Embrace the distraught.*
- Let not disasters frighten. *Tame the waters, and clear the seas.*

Dearest friends:

- This earth is crying out for tending. *Tend it.*
- This earth is sorrowed in its losses and abuses by those who sweep across her for their gain.
- *Clean this earth.*
- *Clean the waters.*
- *Live with humility,* that balance will be restored.
- Take not this earth for granted.

For ignoring the symbiotic relationship of life in all of its forms will result in even more planet-wide catastrophes.

Whereas, *healing* the *stratosphere* will help to renew *all* aspects of the levels of life that nurture this planet *and* all upon her.

To be in this world is to be *one* with the earth, and that means also the airs and the waters.

Dearest ones, this earth is crying out to be nurtured.
Be one who does clean the air, clean the waters, tend the body of Earth.
For this planet is not indestructible, and does not have limitless supplies.
Live humanely to restore the planet.

Dearest friends, I speak as one among you. I speak to assure you that restoration *can* be done, but also that *today* is the time.

- Today, *heal the waters.*
- Today, *heal the stratosphere.*
- Today, in gratitude, *bless the ground* upon which you walk.

Let me say this:

My heart hears you.

My presence is with you.

I know your pain.

This *is* the time to believe, not in ideologies—but in the *Presence* within you that has *always* shown you the way.

This *is* the time to be assured and to remember who *you* were born to be: And now awaken to that, and live it.

I am your beloved. In the world.
Once Jesus. Eternally, Sananda.
With you in the heart. In this moment. On this day.
Let us now rejoice. For, yes, the time *is* now.

Received February 22, 2019

Part II

Return of All the Saints

New messages and meditations

February 23—March 23, 2019

40

The Masters of Light

and Jesus After the Resurrection

Dearest ones, today the Council of Light and I open a new focus of teachings. This is to share more of the Ancient mysteries. Let us, therefore, invite you upon this new look at humanity's long history.

Before I begin, let me affirm that, yes, my presence is in the eternal dimensions—yet *also* I am embodied upon this Earth. For this, let me elaborate.

In the days and millennia after I left the lifetime as Jesus of Nazareth, I have been whole. In the blessings of the Creator, I have been at-one in *The Light.*

Alongside my earthly mother, Mary, and the beloved ones who walked the earth with me in those days, both friends and tormentors, I have become an unfolding presence of the eternal flame of *The All That Is.*

When we of the Earth found our way into the blessed Kingdom, we grew in understanding. All of us.

And, today, each of these splendid souls who gave of themselves for the world is now a Master as well.

The Ascended Masters are many. The Kingdom is filled with the *Light* of holy souls who shed their earthly bodies. This includes all the great Teachers of Earth's history. For we are all of one *Light.* We are all kin.

I speak not for myself. I speak for the Council of Light, which is the known great Teachers of Earth and a multitude more.

We share with you now because of the perilous times on Earth in these days: To help all come to see the incredible beauty that we see in *every* person on the Earth and to see the value in every heart.

We also have come to you, now on the planet—because we are able to embody among you as full adults, while also retaining our *Luminous* Ascended Bodies.

It is not only I who now lives and walks among you. It is *every* great Teacher as well.

The Masters of Light are also embodied on the Earth.

We speak in quiet ways. We do not shine ourselves above others. Yet we are here. In all lands.

It is this you may now see: Every great *Light* who has ever lived *now* walks among you.

Life does not end, my friends. We all continue.

And, dear friends, it is time to embrace in yourselves the humility of reverence, toward all peoples, in all lands. Because every soul is striving to live humanely.

Dearest ones, we of the Council of Light—who once lived on this Earth—are now with you once again.

We do not flaunt ourselves. But we quietly teach, again, in *every* land.

We are seen and known as one of you. We hold not hatred. We spout not vengeance.

Our words are that humanity is now in a moment of *choice:*

- Choose who you will be.
- Choose your words.
- Choose your actions.

For this is how you create peace on Earth.

Peace does not just happen. It is built. One word at a time. One action at a time.

Peace is a choice.

Let me now say, on our behalf, from every great Teacher of Earth's past:

> "Humanity, we love you. We have never left you. And now we beseech you, hear us in your hearts. For we are with you."

Let us now give thanks. For, yes, this *is* the Age. Yes, my dears, this *is* the Age of the Return of All the Saints.

I am your blessed redeemer, once Jesus of Nazareth, now among you—I and my Sisters and Brothers of *The Light*.

I am Sananda, your befriender, always.

Blessed be.

Received February 23, 2019

41
The Creator Angels

The Beginning, and The First E.T.s

This is the Lord. Hello, dearest ones.

It is my purpose to show you how humanity began.

In the beginning was The Void. And in this Void only *The Mind.* And *The Mind* sought companions.

Thus, *The Mind* sent forth Ideas that, then, manifested as Beings of Light, and these are called the angels.

Among these Beings of Light were, and are, seven hierarchies; which are the angels' responsibilities, including: the powers to create.

Thus, the Creator Angels built the worlds; including all the universes, all the cosmos, and all the dimensions.

The Creator Angels then created human beings, in their own form, for *The Mind* sought to build worlds upon worlds.

And on the first world, Perona, also called Eden (or "the first world"), the angels created the first of all human beings.

In this world in the first star system, the Pleiades, the humans became wary of each other. Some (most) were dutiful to *The Light,* their inheritance, and sought only to live with the full memory of their origins.

Yet there were a few who wanted more than they had been given and they sought to take whatever they wished.

The consequence was a planet-wide destruction.

Seeing that this was inevitable, a great portion of these first humans abandoned the lost world and traveled far away, to other star systems: the blue star, in the Orion system; the dog star, in the Sirius system; and in the archer constellation Sagittarius.

The original world Perona (Eden) died in a cataclysmic human-made catastrophe.

The new worlds, three initially, still support human life.

The first to travel to the blue planet, Earth, were from Orion (their ancestors being Pleiadian). Thus, both of those are the largest number of Earth's ancestors.

Today, both of these ancestor worlds are communicating with humans on Earth. Some humans from those worlds even today live on Earth, among the human populations.

Why do I and the Council of Light share this information?

So that you may realize how extraordinary life is.

Eden was not a community on Earth. Eden was the first world.

Humanity did come from Eden, or as it was known, Perona.

Humanity is ancient. You have existed since the beginning of Time, not only Earth time but Time as of all worlds, all universes, all cosmos.

And now, humanity on Earth, it is your time to remember—who you are.

You are from the stars. All humans began in The Void, from a single Thought: *Let there be life.*

I and the Council of Light are preparing you now for the human transformation that is now underway. All humans, in all worlds, are now in *transcension* from third-dimensional bodies to fourth-dimensional bodies.

This is a higher vibratory frequency—of your body and your brain. The result is changes in the human body, including the organ, the brain. This results in higher aptitudes, increased extrasensory abilities, longer lives, and the increasing wisdom of one with a larger brain.

This is now transcending—on Earth, and in all human worlds, of which there are many.

So, my dearest friends, I, once called Jesus of Nazareth, now eternally Sananda, can affirm: You are from the stars.

And now as you are awaking to your greater potentialities, you are learning that war and greed destroy life. Yet comradery and compassion build life and can make you and your world whole.

For this reason, I am now returned. I and all the great Teachers.

We are all embodied, today, on the Earth, to quietly reveal to the multitudes that for your peoples and your lands to be at peace, the only way is to care more for others than for yourselves. For the secret to life is to live with an open heart, toward all.

I am your brother, always, Sananda.

Received February 24, 2019

42

A Greater Destiny

More on Jesus Here Now, and All the Saints, Too

Dearest ones, let this be the day you embrace all in the world. For every person is a part of every other. All that you do and say is a part of every other.

Today, you are immersing yourself in your new deeper self-awareness. This shows you how to be at-one with the people around you and on your path

As you are now aware, we are all connected, in every way.

Our thoughts are a part of the Universal spectrum of all thoughts.

Our actions are a part of the cosmic plan. And our every action implements that plan.

All that we do, with love, is a part of a Greater Destiny awaiting us.

So have no self-recriminations when you feel you have said too much. For every word, spoken in love, is a part of unfolding a Greater Destiny awaiting every person who hears it.

None of us is alone in our lives, in spirit and in body. All of our actions are seen. All we can do is live with an open heart and speak with humility. The rest is a part of a Greater Plan, for all.

Dearest ones, let your heart remain open. Speak with thoughtfulness and kindness. Speak with an open mind and trust in all that is good.

When you do so, only good is the result—in your own life and in the lives of all that you touch.

Today, you are welcomed as a voice of the angels, who work with you in all that you do to make life more wonderful and peaceful for everyone.

In this, I also am with you, in spirit and in body.

I am your befriender, once Jesus of Nazareth, eternally Sananda.

Received February 25, 2019

43

The Great Teachers of Earth

Dearest ones, here we are today with gifts to you from the Brethren of The Light, also called Ascended Masters. We are many.

The Great Teachers of Earth are many more than those identified in history: not only those acknowledged as saints, but many more whose names are lost to the history books and more than those named Mohammed, Buddha, Confucius, and Zoroaster.

Throughout human history, these enlightened minds and hearts have always come into a society to help enlighten the peoples to the truths of how the universe works, and why.

These great thinkers include masters of the arts and sciences, who have changed human thought, such as Einstein and Galileo, Shakespeare and Monet, Nostradamus and Edgar Cayce.

All of these great thinkers and creators were able to access their own great Mind, which is the creative spark accessible to everyone.

Your own higher Mind is a part of you. It is accessible *through* the brain—but is not the brain.

Your higher Mind is the avenue of all new innovations that have altered human perceptions and invented new strategies and tools.

The higher Mind is the tool of inventors in all of the sciences and arts, such as Bill Gates and Steve Jobs; and was the tool of healers who discovered cures for diseases, and those who are still discovering cures.

The arts reveal the spirit of humanity. For it is the creative spark that brings forth beauty—to the eye and to all of the senses.

Music is a gift of the higher Mind, to inspire and also to heal and motivate. In fact, music and the arts exist continuously—through *all* of the higher dimensions, *beyond* physical life.

The beauty and wonders of nature were the first gifts, created by the angels, who also were the first to sing and dance, in the full joy of being. Life has always been felt as wondrous, from the beginning.

So the gifts that humans enjoy were first endowed to the angels, who then bestowed them to human beings, who are of many varieties, in many worlds.

The Great Teachers are masters of spiritual insight. These messengers of *The Light* have many purposes. They are those filled with the deepest love of humanity. They are those who serve beyond themselves and give to others more than themselves. They are healers who seek to ease the suffering and pain of all living creatures. They are *revealers* who share the ancient knowledge of the angels. They are *revealers* who bring new knowledge of the evolving greater Minds.

The Masters of Wisdom have walked this Earth in *every* generation, from humanity's origin, on every world.

And I was one of these.

Today, humanity is in a transformation not ever before experienced since humans were created by the angels. — Until *now*.

Now, my dearest friends—*now*—humanity is in A New Beginning.

Now, all of humanity is undergoing changes in the brain and in the body.

Now, all of humanity is also taking on *new ideas* never before imagined:

- *How* to restore the Earth to her intended majesty.
- *How* to restore humanity's original Intention, as creatures filled with the divine wonders.

Now, all of humanity are awakening to the knowing that *they* are graced with hearts and intellects like unto the angels.

In this awakening is a purpose. And that purpose is to heal humanity's misdirections of the past millennia, which are: hungering for what is not helpful to the one or to the whole, seeking domination over others out of a fear of lack, seeking to destroy any and all living creatures only for the disdain of it, seeking to destroy any and all life forms out of a disregard for all.

These misdirections of appetites in the human behavior are now waning, as the New Multitudes are being born with a respect for all of life and a determination to safeguard the Earth and *all* upon her.

These New Multitudes, being born *now,* reject the hatreds of the past. They rise in great numbers—in every land—to restore equality among the peoples and in all the races.

These New Multitudes are the saints of all the Ages, now returned to the Earth, now defying the egregious torturers who have ruled for eons.

These are all of the saints who have come back to the Earth, not for themselves but for the whole—because the world is in a great need of repair.

And you, my brothers and my sisters, you too have returned to the Earth as a voice of reason to help humanity into its now rightful place in the cosmos.

For though humanity is young among the cosmos, you are now maturing. And it is now time to be adults.

Dearest ones, I speak to you as one of the Teachers who walked upon the Earth:

I am returned already.
I am a man. I am in the body.
I am one, of many.

The New Multitudes being born *now* are the saints of all the Ages, returning also. We are not highly visible. In every land, we live as you do. We are kindred spirits through the higher Mind of *The All That Is*. In that Mind, we commune. In our hearts, we are one in *The Divine That Lives In All*.

And now, en mass, we are here again: In full remembrance of who we were. In full dedication to again give of our insights—to help all of humanity *now* rise up—into your goodness.

For my dears, you are innately good. Each and every one of you. And we are with you, in your lives, in quiet ways, showing the way.

I am your beloved, once Jesus of Nazareth, now returned to you.
Seek me not in the world. I do not come in glory.
Seek me in your heart, where I have always been.

I am with you, always. As are we all.

Touch the spirit of *The Divine* within you and you will hear us and know us. For we are all around you. Even now.

I am your beloved, Sananda.

Received February 26, 2019

44

The Whole That We All Are

Hello, dearest ones, today rejoice. For humanity is arising into the perspective, *"We are all one."*

This is how the world will change. It does take time, millennia. Yet, yes, it has begun.

And we of the Council of Light, and all the angels of the Heavens, are with you with words of encouragement. Because, yes, it is not an easy path.

Yet this *is* a step toward healing:

- Healing hearts of stone.
- Healing minds that are filled with anger and doubt.
- Healing the attitudes that block empathy.

My dearest friends:

- Hold fast to your good heart. For this is your solution—to everything.
- Hold fast to hope. — For *this* sees you through all difficulties.
- Hold fast to courage. — For this is the angel Self of your origin instilling you with actions toward being your full Self, once more.

My dearest friends, all that is in the world—before as well as now unfolding—is a mirror of the whole. For it is the whole that we all are.

Humanity is *one* consciousness. When healing the hatreds, humanity is healing the heart. And that is beginning *now*.

So, beloved, be still and trust what your heart says to you: *Believe.*

Yes, know: It *is* now unfolding.

There is now in the world a new hope, and that is every awakening heart to the realization, *"We are all one."*

I am your befriender, always. Jesus-Sananda.

Received February 27, 2019

45

The First Humans

Before Earth, and The Origin of Angels

Hello, dearest, today I share a secret:

You are truly one of the angels. That is how you began, before the experiment into the denser dimensions.

Now, I am happy to report that all of humanity is, at last, reawakening to the Origin Memory of how all began. It is this that I can now show you.

In the beginning was The Void. And a single Thought. *The Great Mind* was the consciousness that was. Then *The Mind* sought to create benevolent beings in *The Domain* and created the Beings of Light, known to the Earth as angels.

After a Time and a Time again, these splendorous beings grew curious and sought to create a vaster Realm. That was the Origin of all the worlds, in all the universes, in all the dimensions. For the angels were the only beings with a Form, even though of the highest dimension, thus pure *Light,* thus bodies of *Light.*

Then the angels, in their curiosity, began to create the natural wonders. And first on the original worlds, in the Pleiades star system.

One of the worlds was Perona, and it was the first Eden, a land of perfection, with plants and flowers of every imagination, and seas and oceans of every depth.

It was on the first Eden that the angels then created animals, creatures of the earth, the air, and the waters; creatures of great beauty, and also of great intelligence.

Yet still the angels were curious and, filled with delight over their creations, with permission from *The One Great Mind,* they created human beings, who had an intelligence equal to the angels. The first humans not only could speak, they understood the complexities discussed with them by the angels, whom they saw not as gods but as their benefactors.

The first humans and the angels were deeply entrusted to each other, and invested with creating the most beautiful life one could imagine.

These first humans, in harmony with the angels—who manifested them—were the first great thinkers and dreamers in the human species. They were agreeable. They, too, were creative. They, too, were curious.

Then in a Time and a Time again, into this perfect world came a single doubt: What if we are better than the angels? What if they are not our benefactors? What if they created us only for their enjoyment? What about us? What about our own enjoyment? Why can't we do the same? We have the same powers as the angels. We have all the knowledge they have taught us. Isn't it time we did this for ourselves and not for them?

Thus, the first humans created dangerous tools, which resulted in destroying their perfect world. And in the end, in time, there was nothing left. The land was desolate, no longer spectacular or abundant. The waters were filled with the consequences of their poisonous creations. And the beautiful, intelligent creatures of their world were the only food now available.

So the first humans began to dominate all else on their world. Until there was nothing left.

After a Time and a Time again, the first humans devised a way to leave the planet. For it was no longer useful to them. And, thus, began the travels.

This is not a story. This is not a parable. This happened.

Thus, my beloveds, I and the Council of Light—who have lived many physical lives, on many worlds—come to you now to instill what we have learned, not about the cosmos or the origins but about the only thing that matters:

- Appreciate the life you already have.
- Take care of your world.
- Take care of the animals who *share* the world with you, not for your sustenance.
- Take care of each other.

We have learned that the only value in life is in how we treat each other—with *respect.*

This, dearest ones, is the crucial life lesson. Learn this and you will be at peace, regardless of what happens around you.

I am your beloved, once called Jesus, eternally Sananda.

Received February 28, 2019

46

The Splendid Purpose of Being

Yes, dearest ones, life for humanity is—only now—beginning to fulfill the purpose for which all were created.

In this, let there be hope. For the new generations are bringing this gift to you and to us.

In this, let there be fruitful discussion. For the new generations are eager to learn, discern, and expand upon the status quo.

In this, let there be joy. For the new generations are filled with a deep appreciation of all peoples.

Dearest ones, in this world—*now*—you are being taught a new way to see life:

- To see all peoples, of all nations, of all races, as blessed beings created by *The Divine*.
- To see the Earth and all the creatures of the land, air, and seas as blessed beings created by *The Divine*—not to be the sustenance of the humans but to share this world for their beauty.
- To see *all that is* with wonder and respect. For that is the attitude of a precious soul of God. For *all* living creatures, all peoples, and the very Earth itself are perfect creations for the joy and beauty of their existence: Not to be squandered. Not to be discounted. Not to be dominated.

In this, let us lastly say that you, dear *Light,* are a splendorous soul in whom we have much delight. For we of the Council of Light, on Earth and in the Heavens, are filled with joy at the sight of your good heart.

And we can assure you that we are grateful for your attention to learning your own sense of hope and responsibility. We see your attention to the well-being of others and all life. And we are grateful for your place in the world. For you bring fresh eyes.

We share our thoughts only as reminders. Let these teachings merely be tools, to guide and inspire. Not to defame any. Not to demand of any.

Live by your heart, kindly, and by your conscience, thoughtfully, and you will be at peace.

Each day is a new opportunity to express your inner seeing, so that every person might come to feel the splendid purpose of being:

- To love one another.
- To love yourselves.
- To accept one another.
- To accept yourselves.

In this, you are at peace. And for all else, listen within for the counsel of *The Most High,* which is charitable, always.

I am your beloved, with you always, once Jesus of Nazareth, now eternally Sananda.

Received March 1, 2019

47

Political Revolutions

Dearest ones, this is the day of a move forward politically in the hearts of humanity. For tyrants are no longer endured.

The spark of truth awakens a fury among the oppressed, and they will be silent no more, even in the sacrifice of their own lives.

It is a hard thing to do, living under a cloud of brutality. It is a hard thing to do to live under the foot of a dictator. It is even harder to resist and to defy.

But this is now what the peoples in these lands are doing. They are gathering in secret. They are coordinating. They have wise strategies. And now revolutions arise. In numbers not before seen.

It is sad that Earth still hosts tyrants. But these *are* days of *Light* and truth is the victor. Tyrants are facing the brutal *Light* of their own shadows, which haunt them and now will crush their lies.

For there is no freedom of the peoples without truth as their banner.

Unfortunately, this has been the way of the world. Even so, truth will prevail, as it must.

For every person is entitled to personal choice. Every person is entitled to be safe and to know sustenance. Every person is entitled to be loved and valued.

This is the real change being born at last in humanity. The meek are now the soldiers. For they will be silent no more.

These *are* the days long foretold, the days of souls rising. They rise into their personal power, the power of honesty.

The days of abuse are coming to an end. The victories take many lives. — But this seeds the future of humanity.

For the only justice in this world is to defy false leaders, so that the peoples may live in dignity.

Dearest souls, in these "end days" of the tyrannical few is born a new brightness in the world: the human spirit. It is a bright *Light* that each of you already carries within.

And we of the Council of Light, all the Saints of the Ages, all the Teachers of Earth through the millennia, and the angels of all the dimensions—we are now with you on the Earth, in your lives.

We are quietly going about our business—which is to help you see who you are, that you are the new teachers, the new healers, the new wise ones, the new leaders.

You, my friends, are *the new humanity*—born out of the suffering of the Ages, born out of the teachings of those who went before you.

Today, we are merely your counselors, to help you see who *you* are. To show you who *you* are, and why now is the time to believe in yourself, and to be the person you know you came into this life to be: to help others.

Your talents are the doorway. It is now time to trust in yourself. For *every* heart is needed. And you have a wisdom and a kindness unlike any other.

And as you live in the world and do your work, remember: We of the *Light* are all with you, as well.

Be at peace, dear friend. You *are* on the path already.

I am your beloved, one of *The Light,* with you, to help you trust who you already are as you step forward, in faith, in your gifts to the world.

Blessed be.

I am Jesus-Sananda, your brother.

Received March 2, 2019

48

How to Achieve the Life You Dream

and How Jesus Learned That Inner Strength

Dearest ones, be still and know that God is in you. Be still and know that life is evolving, not ending.

Every aspect of life is in evolution, including the human species. That is the body and the brain.

So take heart, and despair not. Live with a gentleness in your spirit. Live with optimism. Live with a refreshed sense of purpose. For the life you dream can be yours:

- When you value others.
- When you value life.
- When you value yourself.

The joy of life is when we do something that is greater than ourselves. That is what motivated me. That is how I persevered. Because what created me was greater than myself. And I felt the power of life in me. And I knew I was here to teach.

You, dearest friends, have your own unique abilities:

- Your life is to serve those you love.
- Your life is to stand full of life.
- Your life is to give words of healing.

In this, you are my brother, my sister. For we are all a part of *The Great Mind* that brought us into life. We are related, dear ones. You and I both began in The Void. We are not separate.

Dearest ones, let your life be a beacon of joy. In this, your own heart is filled with peace, no matter what befalls you.

Give in only to charity. All else is a passing breath. Only a charitable heart taps into the Mind and Heart of God. In this, you discover who you are, eternally, and your reason for choosing this life, at this time, on this Earth.

I am your beloved, once Jesus of Nazareth, now again with you in the world, I am Sananda.

Received March 4, 2019

49
All Creatures Great and Small

and Visitors from the Stars

Hello, dearest souls. This day let us be filled with joy. For we are now immersed in a deep appreciation of life, in all of its forms.

The joy of life is found in appreciating every creature, in every form. We see ourselves in it. We wonder how it feels. Does it think?

By listening and seeing, we come to realize that creature is not an automaton but *does* live not only by its needs but by its wants.

Every creature lives to fulfill not only survival but a happiness in its moments, with others. All creatures have a natural instinct to seek love, not only to fill their bellies.

When we learn to hear them through their behaviors, we learn to see how similar they are to us; not so different really, only in appearance.

This appreciation of all creatures, great and small, teaches us how not to judge our enemies and people who do monstrous things.

The creatures are in the world, by their own right, just as we are. When we learn to hear them and to see them, we are teaching ourselves how to look upon all that is unlike us with a gentleness, with a curiosity, and with a devout appreciation of who they might be, inherently.

This is the grace of life in the physical. It teaches us humility, which is the saving grace of our moments of ingratitude.

Dearest ones, this world hosts many varieties of species. It is not our place to destroy them, any more than it is our right to destroy another human being—who is us.

These life lessons in humility are what prepare us also to meet beings who are like us in attitude but unlike us in appearance.

This is a grand moment, dearest ones. For on the Earth now, and more soon, already there are many like us in heart, who are unlike us in experience *and* unlike us in general appearance.

There are among us—now—hundreds, worldwide, of humans from other star systems. These peoples—The Travelers—live among us, in our lives, in all lands. They number few but they too have jobs, aspirations, and loved ones.

These Travelers are at home here, among us—for they are the ancestors of all on Earth.

So, among us on Earth are not only the Travelers, here to make a home—but also all the saints and masters who once lived on Earth and are now re-embodied as adult awakened human beings, with full awareness and memories of who they are. Yet with new identities in new forms.

So, dearest ones, this vast world is plentiful with beings not like you, yet just as much in appreciation of life as you are. Here to be in this world alongside you, to show the way—to humility.

In humility, we all find our heart open to circumstances we did not expect, and we learn to live free of judgment. And in this now changing global society, the best way to learn to grow with it is in humility.

The humble heart appreciates all.

I, your beloved, am with you, in spirit and in body, Jesus-Sananda.

Let me hold your heart with grace and with love. Call to me whenever you need a friend. I am as near to you as your own breath. Of this you can be sure. For those of us who have returned are also fully *Presence* in our Divine Bodies.

We are *Light*. We are already the Crowning Glory.

And now we bring this to you, quietly, humbly.

Blessed be.

Received March 5, 2019

50

Out of the Waking Sleep

Dearest souls, on this day, humanity is already coming out of the waking sleep. Humanity's heart is being awakened—not to your own troubles but to the troubles of those around you.

You, my dearest, are imbuing your spirit with the angels' prayers for you, that you now will be the whole Self you chose to be in *this* life: Not for yourself alone, but for the hungry and the impoverished. Not for your own success, but to lift up the sorrowed and to teach the young. Not for your own glory, but to heal the pains and disadvantages of those who are lost in mind and have suffered egregious harm.

This is your purpose, dear friend. This is your gift in this life. This is why you *chose* to come—into *this* life, this world, at *this* time.

For, indeed, these *are* the days long foretold. And it takes every good heart to stand in the winds of life and muster courage. It takes every wise heart to stand amidst the suffering and bring a lamp of hope to guide others through their dismay. It takes a prayerful heart to think of others' needs more than one's own.

Dearest soul, this is who you are. And for this, I and the Masters of Wisdom of all the Ages, and the angels of all the dimensions, thank you. For the healing cannot be fulfilled without *your* insight. Your ideas are needed.

We appreciate the challenges you face. For we have been there. Even now, embodied, we see and feel the torments of an Earth life.

We also see and feel the deep goodness and generosity of the human spirit. This is what we see in the many. This is what we feel in you. For you are one of us.

Dearest soul, you once were even more impoverished than most in this world. You once were more disabled than most in this world. You once were more disregarded.

But now you bring your experiences—and healed heart—into this world:

- To lift up those who are abandoned.
- To relieve whose are damaged.
- To instill hope.

That is really all you need to do: Instill hope.

For that is all anyone needs to gather courage. And that is all you need to give.

You, dearest, are a healer—of minds, of spirits. Whatever your tasks and talents, this above all else:

Be a teacher of hope, that others may know their own *Light*—which is peace within. Because once we accept who we are, nothing else can sway us.

You are blessed, dear one. And now you bless life—by simply being the whole Self you already are.

I am your beloved friend, with you always, in spirit and in body, Jesus-Sananda.

Received March 6, 2019

51

The Great Transformation

Dearest ones, let us today lift up others' hopes and know that all in the world is in a change toward healing.

Here, we bring a message from *The Divine:*

> "Let us be glad. For the transformation already has begun.
>
> "Let us be glad. For the hearts of humanity are awakening to their inherent splendor, as a part of *The Whole of All That Was and Is.*
>
> "Let us be glad. For every Mind is awakening to a recognition of higher purpose and, in this, the recognition that all peoples are a part of *The Whole,* and that *all* are a part of The Great Transformation that already has begun."

Dearest ones, *every* person is imbued with the divinity of The Original Beings. *Every* person is innately a part of the angels of all the dimensions. *Every* person is a part of the destiny of humanity.

Not one is forgotten. Not one is left behind. Not one is to be shamed or ridiculed.

For *every* person is an inherent child of God, born of The Origin as an angel, now in human form learning fairness, now in human form learning that justice is kindness and is not hatred.

Dearest souls of all the worlds, *every* person is *now* lifting in hope and in determination toward the Original Selves we all once were: devout, grateful, tempered in joy and generosity.

Lift up your hearts to all that you know you were born to be. Today live your full Self. For that is who you really are.

In the coming days (many), humanity goes through much change and, with this, challenge. The world is not an easy place to be kind, to all. But the world *is* the place to find in yourself your own kind heart, through your own dimensions of goodness.

And when you do, no matter what befalls you, your own life—from that moment on—is filled with the rewards: blessings to you and for you, in all measures.

For all that you seek, it is found when your heart softens and you allow yourself to feel, gently, the pain others suffer. When you do and you reach out to help another, that is when your own needs are abundantly given to you. And abundance is in many forms.

Let us now praise each other. For you and every other around you *is* a part of humanity's Great Transformation, already begun.

I am your beloved, once Jesus of Nazareth, now with you in spirit and in the world. Eternally, I am Sananda.

Received March 8, 2019

52

The Original Worlds

Dearest ones, today humanity is becoming more grateful for the beauty of this Earth and for all the bounty.

Today, let us value the Earth and the creatures. For they also are life, in its multitudes of forms. They, too, live with purpose: to Exist. They, too, revere The Origin, which brought them into life.

Dearest ones, we are all out of The Void. Every living thing was first *not*. Every living thing was first brought into form by the High Beings of Light, the first forms out of *The Consciousness*.

From these first Beings of Light came all. You, me, all the Masters of Wisdom, all of the worlds, all of the creatures, all of the humans.

Humans came into being directly from the High Beings of Light. Humans are the earthly forms of these Beings, given intellect by these Beings.

Always, humans have been the higher-thinking physical species—in all worlds. Not only this one Earth.

There are many Earths, and many types of humans. And all are as you are. And all first came from the Original worlds: first the Pleiades, then Orion, Sirius, and Andromeda. These were the original humans.

And at *this* time in physical history—for the first time since humans were manifest on Perona, out of the creative force—*now,* the entire human species (on all worlds, in all dimensions) are *upleveling* in physical and mental maturity.

This means changes in the genetic makeup, which means increased longevity and increased capacities of the brain. This already has begun, and is seen in children born in *this* century.

Today, I and the Council of Light are embodied on the Earth—so that we are one of you, feeling your pain, knowing your struggles. Because it is now the time of the saints.

This Era just entered (the Age of Aquarius) is the birth of a new kind of human: far-seeing, determined to heal the waters and the earth, respectful of human differences, respectful of the animals.

This new kind of human is endowed with a clearer intellect and is not given to extremes. This new kind of human has a deep appreciation for all that has not been understood and is able to remedy social problems with a clearer eye. This new kind of human is the intended outcome and hope of the greater *Light* that first manifest such examples of themselves into a denser form—for the enjoyment of the beauty given in the worlds.

This is, therefore, the message:

- You were created not to harm others nor to disdain others—but to share with others, in respect.
- Your task in life is to heal the wounds of all that suffer, and to live without hatred.
- Your task in life is to value all that you have and not to harbor jealousy for what you do not have. For when your heart is open to being kind, all that you require comes to you: sustenance and security.

It is this that I am teaching in these new books. And for this, I am always with you, for counsel in spirit and in the body.

I am your befriender, once called Jesus of Nazareth, eternally I am Sananda.

Received March 10, 2019

53

The Holy Spirit

Hello, dearest friends, *The Divine* is heard through our own devout sweetness. Hear now in your own heart:

> "Dearest ones, this is the Universal I AM.
>
> "It is in this higher level of focus that you are able to hear *The Divine* speaking in your own mind *to* you.
>
> "It is in this deep connection with *The Divine* that you are able to receive the thoughts of Ascended Masters and angels.
>
> "It is in this reverence toward life that you are able to be blessed with a true respect for all peoples."

Dearest friends, I—the one you have known as Jesus—*am more than one consciousness*. My presence is Whole and, thus, *I am in all lands and in all open hearts*.

My words come to you in the small tender voice you feel in your heart, your soul, but hear as thoughts *to* you inside your mind.

This is the form of speech *also called the Holy Spirit*. The angels always have spoken in this way, when they imbue you with their love.

This is *also telepathic communication,* as all Beings of Light have always spoken to humanity.

I, too, speak in this way, when you listen with reverence for the voice of God.

For my dearest, God is in all of us—and in all of you. We are all a part of *The One Great Mind*. And we are able to hear the impressions from that *Great Consciousness* that created all.

Now, dearest, listen in your own heart, with reverence, to *The One Divine* now speaking to you:

> "Hello, my *Lights* who are myself in form. You are now awakening—not to who I AM but to who you are.
>
> "Dearest, you are imbued with the ability to hear the angels.

"As you now hear my thoughts to you, in your own mind, now be still . . . and allow *The Divine* to fill you with the love of all. For that is *how* you hear my words and that is *how* you know me, *within*.

. . . .

. . . .

. . . .

. . . .

"Be still now. . . . And let my love for you wash over you. For I am here, and I am always with you, as your counsel, as your friend. In your arms, as you are in mine."

. . . .

. . . .

. . . .

. . . .

Received March 11, 2019

54
The Keys to Happiness

Dearest soul, good morning! What a beautiful day!

- Live to be a blessing, and your days will be blessed.
- Live with a generous heart, and abundance will fill your life.
- Live to be kind, and kindness will be shown to you.

These are the keys to happiness.

Happiness is a heart at peace. Happiness is knowing you are a good person, doing your best every day. Happiness is living with forgiveness, of your own mistakes and the mistakes of others.

- Keep your heart open and you will find your way.
- Keep your heart free of judgments and you will be quiet in your nights.
- Keep your heart full of respect and you will be respected.

Yes, it is true. Do unto others as you would have them do unto you.

This is a day to rejoice—and your days will be filled with joy, *within*.

No matter what befalls you in this world, joy in your heart is a lightness that cannot be taken from you. In this is your peace of mind.

Blessed be. I am Jesus-Sananda.

Received March 12, 2019

55
The Angels' Archives

The Teachings of Love

Dearest ones, in this book we of the Council of Light and the angels are bringing forth the teachings from the hidden archives, hidden only to those who have not yet awakened to the tremendous inner connection with *The All That Is.*

Let us now reveal that humanity came from the angels. Every one of us was first an angel. For they were the first manifested into form—as Beings of Light—out of The Void, by the *One Consciousness* that pervades all that is, ever was, and ever will be.

As angels incarnated to worlds such as Earth, it is our responsibility to uphold the best of our purpose, which is:

- To care for all others, according to their needs to survive and to be whole in body, and
- According to our talents, which are unique to each of us.

Dearest ones, let the life of God be your life. Let the love of all be what you bring forth into the world, through your own splendid gifts—of music, of words, of hands that heal.

For you are in this world not for yourself alone—but for those whose lives you help, to the better.

This world is not an easy existence, for anyone. And those who are able to live above their struggles are the teachers who bring *Light* in their words and in their example.

This is what I wish for you: that you be your best self, as an example of love, which is the life force that binds everything together.

It is through love that we are one body and one mind.

- For in love, we are able to forgive.
- In love, we are able to be gentle instead of harsh.
- In love, we are able to be leaders, because we see all clearly.
- In love, we care more for the well-being of all than for our own troubles.

In this, what to do becomes clear in your mind. Then all you need do is pursue it, with dedication.

That is the secret to life. For a heart that is filled with purpose is a heart open to learn, and ready to give. And that is who *you* are.

I am your beloved, Jesus-Sananda.

Received March 16, 2019

56

All the Prophecies Are Now Coming to Bear

The universe is expanding. It does not end.
Nor does life end.
Life on Earths continues. All Earths.
Humanity continues, in all worlds.

Now, dearest friends—*now*—Earth is transcending into fourth-dimension physical. This is an astronomical event. It is a higher vibratory frequency.

This is the New Earth prophesied.

In addition to Earth, *all* physical worlds, in all universes, are transcending as well. All life.

This means that *all* of humanity are also transcending *now*.

The fourth-dimension physical changes the molecular structure of the body. This results in increased longevity, more cures—through science—and that is because of an increased brain capacity.

All humans are already—now—in *transcension*. The younger generations, especially those born since 2001, are the new healers and visionaries. You are the new world leaders. Now.

Those born since the 1970s also have the new genetic makeup. These are those with open minds, who teach and prepare the way.

It is in *this* Age of life that all the prophecies are now coming to bear.

This is why *all* the saints and Masters of Wisdom—of this Earth—are now embodied on *this* Earth, to show the way.

We are here. In bodies pure.

Here is the important message:

- Listen to your own heart for the truth. Your own instincts tell you who is a pure teacher—and who is him or herself misguided or confused.
- Follow not any. Follow only your own heart. Follow only what is good. Follow only what is fair.
- Live only for what is fair—to all and for all.

This also is the way of those who are pure.

Thus, you must be discerning.

- Do not blindly accept the miscreants who cry foul.
- Do not blindly follow bright words and promises.
- For your own sake, trust only those who are gentle of heart and kind in their words.
- Trust only those who teach cooperation and inclusion, of all.

For the pure leaders are those with open minds and whose actions are goodwill toward *all.*

Any who says that only he or she can lead you speaks not truth.

You—in yourself—already know what is true. Trust your own knowing. *That* is *The Divine* in you, guiding you.

Do not be swayed by bright promises. Listen to your own reason.

This is why I am here again, now. As before I warned of false prophets, again I come to do so. Because I know that *The Divine* is within *every* person—every person of every faith, every religion, every race.

Judge not any other. For that other is a reflection of you.

Live only the best person *you* are. Be that person *now,* today.

That is how *you* help to shape the world into the global society it was always meant to be.

Earth always was intended to be *one* world, with one peoples.

Dearest friends, the *Light* of all angels surrounds you now. Be a blessing. That is the only task. That is the only purpose. Be a blessing.

I am your beloved, Jesus-Sananda.

Received March 18, 2019

57

We Are Here For You

Dearest humanity, we of the Council of Light are today with you in the world. We are in simple jobs, going about our lives humbly, sharing the peace we carry within. We are round about you, in your daily lives.

- Be at peace, dear souls, not for our sake—but for your own.
- Be at peace in your mind—that you may remember who you are in your eternal essence, and let that be the *Light* you share with the world.
- Be at peace in your thoughts—that you may reflect calm in your words and actions.
- Be at peace in your words—that you may reveal calm of spirit to all around you.
- Be at peace in your actions—that you may be a leader with goodwill as your lamp.

These are the strengths of anyone who seeks to be useful. These are the strengths of anyone who cherishes life and seeks to lift up others out of despair.

You, dear souls, have come into this life—not for your own appetites and will but to lift up all who struggle. You are in this life—not for your own pleasures but to be an example of an open heart, that others may find gratitude in their own deep regrets.

For when we are able to be grateful for what we have, then we are free of the burdens that others would place upon us. *This* is how we let go of judgment.

Gratitude is the healer of all that wounds us.

- Live in gratitude, and your life is free of regret.
- Live in gratitude, and your heart is free from sorrow.
- Live in gratitude, and your mind is free to fly.

Dearest souls, I and all the Masters of Light are in the world—*today*. In new adult bodies. Embodied. Fully aware of who we were and are.

We are here for you.

Not for you to worship us. For we are teachers in simple ways. Not for you to adulate us—but to realize that you, too, have the glorious *Light* in you.

Dear friends, we are abundant among you, in your daily lives—that you will feel the power of love, which restores hope. For in hope, all things are possible.

- In hope, you touch God in you.
- In hope, your eyes are open to the fruits of goodness in spirit.
- In hope, your ears are open to the whispers of the angels and the Masters of Wisdom.
- For in hope, you are a *Light* awakened to your own joyous true Self: an embodied angel, ready to live as you were born to be.

Blessings to you, dear friend, in all that you do from this day forward. For you are a *Light* in the world. And the world needs you.

Your family needs you. Your enemies need you—as the *Light* you are.

I am your beloved, always with you.

No matter your faith or religion or if you have none, I am your befriender in all that you seek to be in life. For a good life is when we live to be of help. And you, my friend, have chosen to live in *this* time. You are in the world—*now*—because life is changing and you can be an influence of goodness.

In this, feel the presence of the angels, the Blessed Ones, and the Masters of Wisdom who were once on this Earth. For we are your counselors, in every corner of the Earth.

Blessed be. I am Sananda.

Received March 21, 2019

58

Now Is the Age Prophesied

Dearest ones, I am completing this message on Return of All the Saints.

Simply know that as promised by my forebears and predecessors—the prophets Elijah, Samuel, and Jeremiah—and as foreseen by the spiritual teachers and leaders of the Age since I lived as Jesus of Nazareth, and by my own words at that time as well:

Yes, dear friends, this time now on Earth *is* the Age prophesied. You *are* in what was called "The End Times," meaning "the end of *time*" as experienced in third-dimensional frequencies.

- You *are* living in "the last days," meaning the last days of the third-dimensional frequency.
- You *are* now surrounded by the adult-embodied Masters of Light, known as the Ascended Masters, who include all the revered Teachers of humanity's history, including myself.
- You *are* surrounded by a multitude of angels of the higher dimensions, embodied as guides and counselors.
- You *are* surrounded by the spiritual dimensions of the higher vibratory frequencies, which now are merging with the world you have known.
- And you *are* sharing this world also with beings embodied from higher dimensions and from other worlds.

My dearest friends, *now* your lives are splendidly supported in serenity and goodwill. Whatever your personal struggles, know that help is all around you.

Reach out.

Listen.

Accept the hands that offer you relief.

And listen within, wherein the counsel of the Masters is available to you.

For we have been where you are. We know your hardships and your challenges.

We also know that the higher dimensions are only a breath away.

We are in your midst, now, today. We walk among you—in the world—as men and women, of all races and appearances.

You can know us by our peaceful presentations. We are not judges. We are not filled with anger or retribution. We bring hope and insight.

Our voices are what your own heart tells you:

- Be kind to others.
- Be a blessing in life.
- This is the central teaching.

We all love you. We see you. We hear you.

And now have faith in your own insights, as well. For *you* chose to be in *this* life at *this* time in human history. *You* are here because of your own unique ideas and solutions. You see the problems and you bring help.

And dear ones, your help is needed.

Be assured, life is now upleveling. And you are one of those bringing encouragement. All you need to focus on, in all that you do, wherever you are, whoever you are, is to live to be a blessing.

- In this is the quiet mind.
- In this is the peaceful heart.
- And in this you are able to know—who you are, why you are here, and what to do next.

Thank you for allowing me into your day.

I am with you always, Jesus-Sananda, the *Light* of God.

Received March 23, 2019

Part III

There Once Was a Girl

New messages, parables, and meditations

March 25—June 23, 2019

59
I Invite You to Take This Journey with Me

The universal consciousness *is* the Divine Mind. *Is* God.

This is how we hear the angels.

This is how we hear *the still small voice within.*

We all have access to this Greater Mind. It is the Universal Mind—of which we are all a part.

This Part III is an exploration of consciousness: What it is, how we are all consciousness, and how we are all a part of a single *group* consciousness.

This Part reveals how everything that exists came from *The One Mind*, a consciousness that pervades all worlds and all dimensions, and created everything in the visible world out of The Nothingness.

This Part thus explores the nature of all life, the origin of all life, the nature of God manifest, and how all that exists came from a single Consciousness.[4]

I am Sananda. One of my physical lives was Jesus of Nazareth.

But we all have lived many lives. And in this Part III, I explore how and why we exist, where we came from, and how we came to be. This Part reveals the true eternal nature of our souls, and what our soul is.

I welcome you to take this journey with me.

I am your friend forever, in life and in your spiritual center, which is the core of you.

Always, I am Sananda.

Received March 25, 2019

[4] See more on what is consciousness and what is God in upcoming book *The Divine Code in Us*. In addition, more on the origin of all life and how all came to exist is addressed in *Humanity 2.0: The New Humanity*, *The Soul Path*, and in a future book *The Angels of Serendipity*.

60
What Is Your Potential in Life?

Hello, dear souls. Do you know who you really are? Did you know that you were born whole?

- You were born with an open heart, ready to give to others.
- You were born with an open mind, ready to learn more and be more.
- You were born without hatred.

Dearest ones, you are not the fears that hide behind your worry. You are not the rage that flaunts itself through you when you are afraid.

No. Instead, you are able to be all-seeing. This means that you can see who you were born to be: a good influence in the world. And you can see who others were meant to be: their full potential.

So, what is your potential in life? It is:

- To let go of the drama that weighs you down.
- To let go of the regrets that shadow the you who is a blessing in life.
- To let go of the terrors that haunt you—and, instead, stand up against all that terrorizes you.

Dearest friends, your potential is to live fully from a heart that is free of bitterness. To live fully from a mind that is free of judgment. To live fully from a place of goodwill in every word and every action.

- Power is not in violence.
- Power is not in cruelty.
- Power is not in rage against what you don't understand.

My dearest friends:

- The real power is in being able to see who others really are—and seeing and feeling who you really are, underneath your uncertainties.
- The real power is in lifting yourself up, and in lifting up others. When you do this, you rise out of the past hurts and you create a new reality for yourself, on Earth.

- The real power is in bestowing kindness upon all that you see.
- The real power is in forgiving others' lack of kindness.
- The real power is in coming to your own inner stillness.

For when you are calm within, the world is less foreboding.

When you are calm within, answers arise easily in your heart.

When you are calm within, you do not distress over the pains in the world.

When you are calm within, you know who you are and who you were born to be. You know the hour's purpose. You know the year's purpose. You know your own life's purpose.

And this knowing guides your choices . . . and the right choices ease your life and ease your mind.

Dearest one, you already are who you believe you can be. That is who you already are—*now*.

I am your beloved, Sananda, once known as Jesus of Nazareth, now and always eternal.

As are you.

Received April 2, 2019

61

Why the Push–Pull in Life?

Hello, dearest ones. Today we explore the meaning of life's lessons. On the Earth, we are bombarded by experiences that challenge us: We are hurt, we hurt. We are angered, we are angry against. We are slighted, we slight.

This push–pull tests our mettle and helps us to see who we are and who we can be.

These life challenges reveal what we have learned as a soul and how we are increasing in our abilities to see truth in all peoples.

Life is filled with an abundance of sadness. It is also filled with joy. Life in the physical is a constant flow between what we are and what we can be.

Let us now rise up into our better Selves, so that we can bear more easily the onslaughts of others' errors in judgment.

Let us be who we are, fully, without regret.

Let us uphold honesty in every word we speak. For all that we truly have is our own words and our own perceptions.

When we are able to be genuine with others, that is when we are truly free. For a heart that is free of secrets is a free life, and a mind that is free of bias is a free life.

We are free—in ourselves—only when we are able to rise in our empathy.

Empathy is our teacher and is also our healer.

Empathy shows us what must be fixed and also how to fix it.

With empathy, we are able to rise out of our own grievances and let others be who they are, without ourselves being angry.

Empathy is a tool not only of the human being. It is a trait of the soul. The soul is our eternal Self. It is who we are—beyond the personality.

Our soul is our Original Self, the being we have been since our beginning. Our soul is our inherent capacity.

This, then, is the greatest life lesson: to fully be our soul in the world.

In this way, we live a blessed life and, in this way, we are a blessing to others.

The only real purpose of life is to live as a holy one. — And that is one who is free of anger. That is one who is free of bias.

When we are able to live in our Soul Self—that is when we have risen above the biases of the world. That, then, is when we are a gift to the world. And, in this, a gift to our own being.

I am your beloved, once Jesus of Nazareth. Today and always, I am Sananda.

Received April 7, 2019

62

Hope and Courage Feed Your Life

Your Mind Is Your Own

Hello, dearest ones. Greetings on this beautiful day. Today, let us learn who we are, in essence:

- We are mind—that which directs our ideas.
- We are spirit—that which guides our drives to serve.
- We are the counsel of the angels, in our voice and teachings.
- We are the higher wisdoms manifest.

Dearest friends, we are not our body. Our body is our vehicle.

In all the dimensions of life, our body is a variable. However, our mind and spirit, these are constants.

So, no matter the shape of your body, nurture the feelings and thoughts that feed it and heal it. For it is what we *think* that gives our body what it needs to support us.

Dearest, all that is was first *thought*. So, how we think does affect the shape of our body.

In the current world, bodies vary in shape and color. But your *mind* is your own. It is your unique identity—that has always been *you*.

You have unique ways of being who you are. No one else has your insights and vision. No one else is *your* voice and your ideas. Your mind is your own.

Therefore, above all:

- Be a whole mind by tending to what nurtures your spirit and tenders love to others.
- Be a whole mind by treating your spirit with the affection it seeks—to be kind, to help, to support.
- Be a whole mind by accepting that your spirit is the eternal you and is the part of you that is most visible to others . . . when you live unencumbered by fear.

Dearest, you are your mind, the part of you that creates.

You are your spirit, the part of you that dreams, searches, thrives, and gives.

These are the Self who lives forever and is unbound by circumstances.

These are the Self who lifts up all others with hope, and shows others how to be courageous.

Courage is of the spirit. Hope is of the mind. These are life—and are the food for which you yearn.

- Live for this, and the rest will be in your life.
- Live to give hope, and hope will be in your own life.
- Live to be courage, and courage will be in our own emotions. For courage is innate in you. You already have it.

Hope is the spirit of life—filling you with joy and a heart that cares. For when you care, and you give of yourself to help others, hope is the promise given not only to them but to yourself.

Dearest one, live to be helpful and you will realize that what most matters is already in you.

You find it when you stand up and show the goodness that you are, innately.

You are not your circumstances. *You* are a bright *Light* of hope, standing in faith and acting in courage, for the good of all.

This is your freedom. *This* is your peace. *This* is your place in the world.

I am your beloved, once Jesus of Nazareth. Eternally I am Sananda.

Received April 10, 2019

63

There Once Was a Girl

a Story

Dearest ones, your life is an opportunity to become the full presence of *Light* you were born to be.

You are already drawn to the service of your talents, innate in you, to be shared with all.

Now fully embrace and give all of yourself to it. For that is why you are here. That is the Big you, born to be in this world—now, at *this* time, *where* you are.

Now, I bless you: This time in human history needs your insight. This Era in human expansion needs *your* voice.

Use your heart's call. Listen to your heart's call within. This is what you were born to be and do.

Everything in life is about learning gratitude, and this teaches you humility—which teaches you grace.

Remember, you *are* your heart's call. This is your true Nature. Whatever happens in your life—around you, to you, to your mind, to your body—*you* are still your eternal Self, who *is* always in the *Light* of Divine grace.

You are the *Light* in the world who can help to heal others' sorrow or confusion. *You.*

Let us now share a story:

> There once was a girl who felt unwanted and unloved—and unlovable. She believed this because her parents had told her so.
>
> Through abuses to her spirit—as a child, then as a woman—she struggled to hold onto hope. Despite the anguish and sorrow she carried, always uncertain, in her deep inner-knowing place—her core—she *knew* she was more than she had been told, repeatedly. She *knew* she had something beautiful inside of her to offer.
>
> So, she persevered. She followed her mind's quest to learn more. She listened to her heart's yearning to discover more—about her true inner nature.

Listening and acting upon her heart's whispers toward the *Good* in her, she persevered.

She learned to trust the inner counsel. She learned to understand the counsel, as if her soul was guiding her. She learned to intuit *and* to discern. She learned to *see* with her heart's wisdom, to see truth and to *feel* truth.

These sensibilities expanded the more she used them, every day.

Then came the day when a Clarity came upon her, in the stillness of the night—as if an angel's *Light* surrounding her and imbuing her with the wisdom of The Highest, The Divine.

This new awareness became the path of the rest of her life. And led her—always by her heart's recognition—toward how to give to others what she herself was learning.

She honed her talents. She gave herself to them—knowing *this* was what she was meant to do. And knowing no more than that, she persisted.

And then the talents bore fruit.

Today, that uncertain little girl, that uncertain woman, listens to the soul's counsel within for everything that is her path—of *service.*

Today, though she still has self-doubts and she still has human frustrations with life's events, she focuses (and refocuses) on the task at hand: *How today do I serve?*

This is the guiding *Light.*

Dearest ones, this is the story of many—both girls and boys. Being in the world is a place . . .

- *First,* to discover who you are.
- *Second,* who you can be.
- *Third,* to be it.

Being in the world is a place to prosper in peace of mind, in serenity—at your core—regardless of the inevitable bouts of uncertainty or impatience.

Focus on the best part of you—and all else will fall into balance with it.

First follow and live by your heart's call. All else, then, will become clear to you. One step at a time.

I am your beloved, once Jesus of Nazareth. Now eternally, Sananda.
I am with you, always, in spirit and in body.
I see you. I know you.
Now know yourself.

Received April 15, 2019

64
Restoring Your Innocent Joy

Dearest humanity, let us today reach out to help another, in some way.

Goodwill is what heals the dysfunctions in peoples and between peoples. Goodwill heals wounds between peoples and between nations.

When we are able to drop our pretentious pouts and *hear* the others, we are also learning to heal ourselves of our own deep fears.

Let not fear block your peace of mind. Let not fear abandon your hope.

You, my dearest, are today already loved.

Let me share a story.

> There once was a girl who felt abandoned and, in truth, she was. She also was hurt, deeply, by those who were her parents and grandparents. Instead of loving her, they judged her and sent her away, not for her own faults but for their own. In their fears of their own failures, they sent her away.
>
> And she spent all of her life, into old age, still affected by their inability to cherish her.
>
> Dearest friends, this girl, then woman, then elder, was always shadowed by the loss of her young faith in those who were supposed to love her. And though she learned to believe in herself as a self who is kind, she still carries this old wound.

Dearest friends, the wounds of childhood are difficult to release. Yet coming to know your true Self—as a genuinely caring person—helps to heal and clear the old sadness.

Sadness in one's psyche is a burden. — But you can let go of its teeth upon your hope.

Goodwill is the salve.

When you are able to let go of your resentment, *that* is when you begin to truly believe in yourself again.

When you are able to let go of hating those who have hurt you—truly let go of any remorse—*that* is when you are able to renew the innocent joy of the child you once were.

My dearest, faith in yourself—with innocent joy—heals your sadness of the years.

You restore that faith through allowing a heart of goodwill to nurture within you.

Let not the past damage your faith in the *Light* you are. Live from the fulfilled gratitude that is rebirthed in you . . . from *every* kind action and every thought of goodwill.

Goodwill heals you—deeply—*every* time you *feel* it.

So let your heart release to the inherent good in you.

Every time you release, you are healing yourself . . . and restoring the inherent innocent joy.

As is the girl.

I am your beloved. Always with you, in spirit and in body. I am Jesus-Sananda.

Blessed be.

Received April 18, 2019

65

The New *Be-Attitudes*

Hello, dearest ones. Today, I show you the Kingdoms of Heaven. For they are filled with your loved ones, and all the Beings of Light who speak into your heart.

The angels are round about you, at all times—in your lives and in your dreams.

They whisper into your mind the advice you need for what to do or not do to fulfill your life and to know your way.

They whisper into your mind the counsel to your prayers and the insights to your expanding thoughts.

They tender your heart to the Unseen and prepare you for all the Higher Teachings, such as I now am bringing to you now.

Dearest ones, I too counsel you in your heart, to . . .

- Love one another.
- Be kind to those who live in fear and terror.
- Be kind to those who tread in the world with foreboding.
- Be kind to those whose hearts are still asleep.
- Be kind to those who shirk their responsibilities.
- Be kind to those who hinder the path of goodwill.

These new *Beatitudes* are not to say you must recklessly allow others to be cruel. All cruelty must be abated.

Rather, stop assaults. — But do so without resentment. Do so without hatred.

Yes, halt cruelty and thievery in *all* of its forms. And halt the abusers of justice and those who defy others' their right to freedom. — But do so without harboring ill-will. Do so without carrying vengeance.

Dearest, the point is:

- Yourself be free of darkness. — But, yes, put a plug in it wherever you see it.

- Yourself carry not anger. — But, yes, block all actions of hatred and vile despicable cruelty.
- Yes, reprimand those who kill and maim. — But do so without carrying delight in their suffering.
- Neither cause suffering, nor reward it.
- Neither carry violence, nor perpetrate it.
- Instead, be steadfast against all injustices *and* in your own mind and heart.
- *This* is the way to tender a reckoning to those who unleash their fury, without yourself being enraged.
- In your own heart, be *still*.

Dearest, these new *Beatitudes* are to clarify what it means to release hardness in yourself, yet also address any others' abuses.

Give not freedom to any who tortures. — But do that without yourself being blinded by your own distaste for their blunt actions.

Harden not your own heart, even as you render such hardness in others. — And be not abusive yourself.

This is how you keep your own heart free of damage, and how you free your mind of what has haunted you.

You are *Light*. Be the *Light* you are.

Yes, shine *Light* on all that is troubling. — But bring not those troubles into yourself.

Lift up those who are aggrieved. — But bring not those egregious torments into yourself.

Be the *Light* of the angels, in your counsel and in your remedies. Be the *Light* of the angels as you rectify all that is unjust. — But bring not injustice into your own actions and words.

Dearest, you are my friend in the world. Let my voice and the voices of angels *light* your way. Let us lift your worries. For we are always with you.

Whenever you are unsure of what to do: Pause and allow the wisdom to come into you. In that, you can *know* and there is no doubt.

The wisdom is available to you. It is in the tender stillness within. In that stillness is the voice of *The Divine* guiding you.

I am with you always. Once Jesus of Nazareth, I am eternally Sananda. Blessed be.

Received April 23, 2019

66

The Good You Feel Is in You

Jesus Reflects on His Own Human Challenges

Dearest ones, you are each one of *The All.* You are not separate from God. You are one of *The Great Mind.* You are not separate from the angels. You are one of *The All That Is.* You are not separate from the world and the life you see around you.

Dearest ones, all of humanity are a part of a single *Mind.* All of humanity are a part of a whole sensory body of *Thought.* All of humanity are a part of *One Consciousness.* You and we are all a part of a *Single Force of Energy.*

Dearest ones, we may think we are separate—but we are all *One Force of Energy,* which is our combined attitudes.

We *are* our attitudes.

Life is an external expression of what we feel. If we feel lost, we see all who are destitute as reflections of ourselves. If we feel humble, we see all who are kind and helpful to others—because that is who we are.

Live not to be someone else. Be who *you* truly are in your own esteemed views that lift you up. Be who *you* truly are in your own deep gratitude for what you have.

Life is not for, "Give me. Give me. Give me."

Life is for, "I see you. I honor you. I help you."

You are in life to be all you can be. You were born in *Light,* and *Light* is what you are.

Embrace your inner good. This is what frees your heart and mind. When you live the good you are, that is when you are free.

> Dearest ones, I have been troubled. I have been sorrowed. I have been abandoned. Yet I came to see that is not the self I was born and able to be.
>
> I am not saying it is easy to let go of fear or judgment or doubt. I am not saying it is easy to forgive those who assault you.
>
> But I am saying it can be done. And I am saying that when you are able to lift yourself out of your own regrets—through self-

> forgiveness—that is when you are no longer bound by the platitudes of those in the world who walk blindly and without gratitude.

You, my dearest, are *already* able to let go of the hostilities that have bound you. You are already able to accept a gentler path in yourself.

I am not saying that means to let others hurt you. I am only saying that a gentle spirit is able to slough off others' cruel natures. A gentle spirit is able to slough off others' indignity or rage.

Yes, in life, there are times of horrible injustices, and you may feel it is futile even to try to be the good you feel is in you.

Yet, my dearest, that good is the very thing that will free you . . . and teach you that the world is *not* all terror and cruelty. When you are able to trust yourself in your own instincts, that is what lifts you out of despair.

You, my dearest, are greater in heart than you ever imagined you could be. I see this in you. I see you as you are, innately. *This* is how I am able to love you, no matter who you are. I see you as you were born and which is your innate ability to be. *Now*. In *this* life.

You are not what torments you. Be the good that is in you. Trust yourself. *This* is how you change your life.

My dears, all of us go through moments of hesitation. Every great Teacher has such moments. The only thing that changed us—and changed the course of our lives—is that we learned how to stop our self-doubts. We learned how to let go of hatred. We learned how to *feel* the truth of our own potential: the good in us.

Wisdom is born out of goodness coming into action, in the heart.

You, too, are just like us, like me. You are no different. For you, my dear, are also an angel incarnate.

Live as the angel you once were. Remember the *feeling* of your open heart. *Feel* the truth of you. You are more than your daily routines. You are not your worries.

Be *all* that is in you. Live the good that is in you. All else comes from this.

I am your beloved, once Jesus of Nazareth, eternally I am Sananda.

Received April 29, 2019

67

The New Way Now Building in Humanity

Dearest ones, this is a day to believe—in yourself, in your talents, in the opportunities coming to you now.

Let this be the day you embrace the abilities given to you both by birth and by spirit. For it is not by chance that you dream and are drawn to *The Light.*

This world is undergoing tremendous changes. And though it is filled with loss and destruction and cruelty, these are not the new way that is now building in humanity.

For you are now able to see and touch the deeper realities, which until now have been inaccessible to most.

Now, dear ones—*now*—all of humanity have direct access to the *Divine Mind* and no longer require an intercessor.

Forgiveness is in one's own heart. You are not beholden to anyone who tells you that they are the only way. For peace is found—and lived—in your own conscience.

Conscience is the new word for how to live a good life. It is already in you to know right from wrong. When you ignore your innate sense of this, that is when you bear the consequences.

Live by your own innate knowing of what is best for all, and it is also best for you. For peace in your mind and feelings is the value and reward of living with good in your thoughts and desires. How do you do this, in this busy world?

Pause.

Be still.

Slow down.

Make time to be still, and to listen.

The world is always active. When you make time to let go of that for a while, that is when you begin to restore and refresh.

Balance in your moments is how to find restoration of the inner calm. Let not the world's activities distract you. Choose how you are in the world.

Live first to find and nurture your inner calm, and the rest will be more easily managed . . . and enjoyed.

True joy is found in the calmness of still moments—and in living that for others.

Being present is how you let go of the distractions. Being present is how you let go of the interferences being a bother.

Life is full of needs. Life is also full of choices.

Choose how you spend your time. Choose time to be *still,* in which your mind *stills,* your emotions *still,* and your breath *stills.*

In the *still* breath, now release.

Let go.

Be in the breath now, and all finds its balance.

I am your friend, always. Jesus, the *Light* of the world. Eternally, I am Sananda.

Received April 30, 2019

68

The Eighteen Principles

Jesus Shares the First Lessons He Learned As a Boy

Good morning, dearest. Let us today discuss the purpose of your life. How do you know why you are here? How do you know the meaning of life? All the answers we seek are within our hearts.

This is the first lesson I learned as a boy when I was Jesus of Nazareth. As we studied the Ancient masters' teachings, we learned the principles of meditation, which are:

- To be still in body.
- To quieten the mind through rhythmic breathing.
- To slow the thoughts gently and without rushing.
- To quieten our emotions by allowing the peace to fill us.
- To let go of all around us until we are only in the moment.
- To surrender our personal choices to the divine will within us.
- To be still in that gentle, kind surrender only to the good.
- To allow our feelings to relax and our mind to flow.

In this, our mind begins to receive the whispering of angels.
In this listening comes the soft gentle words of hope.
Then forgiveness.
Then how to proceed in our next moment.

After this, words come to us that are from *beyond* our own understanding, learning, and reading.

Words come to us that we *feel* are new ways of seeing life, the world, and who we are.

These words touch us spiritually like a healing balm. They soothe us. They restore us. They raise us up. They revere us and also guide us.

In this state, we then feel the grace of *The Divine* imbuing our mind s thoughts, filling our being and body with a luminous vibrant energy.

It is at once healing and nurturing.
It is at once uplifting and expanding.

In the *Light* from *The Divine*, we feel ourselves as if born anew.

We feel enlightened with ideas that stretch our wisdom.

We feel enraptured with a crescendo of emotions that are splendorous.

We feel the saintly presence of the angels of all the Heavens and the Masters of Wisdom who have gone before us—the great healers of the world, the great thinkers, the great teachers.

And as we are filled with the *Light* of *The Divine*, the great teachings fill us. Not in words, but in an eternal understanding. Not in thoughts, but in a new inborn wisdom.

In this, we elevate—to our Original Nature, when we first were an angel. And we *remember.*

We remember our origin. We remember The Origin.

We remember The Beginning. We remember *The One Great Consciousness* that gave life to all.

In this, we are one with all life. In remembering, we restore our connection with our original Intention: to be *Light,* to serve *The Light,* and to live the *Light* in *all* that we do and say.

My dearest, when we learn to imbibe the *Spirit of All Life* into our being, we are on the threshold of restoring our Original Self—while here in the body, while physical.

Humans are not perfect. Angels are.

Saints are not perfect—but they *are* akin to the angels they once were.

I was not perfect, but I did discover the inner perfection to which we all strive: my Original Self.

And in that moment, I realized, *This is who I Am. This is who we all are.*

And in *that* moment, that is when I knew—and remembered, *This is why we are all here, and how we get back to the pure Love we once were.*

My dearest, when we open our heart to the Divine Love that pervades *all* of life, we are imbuing the angelic frequency of our Original Self.

This is how we rise above human sadness. *This* is how we learn to forgive those who torture and torment. *This* is how we let go of hatred and fear.

We feel the Divine Love *in* us. We allow the Divine Love to restore us and teach us:

- We are not in life to wallow away in our sorrows.
- We are in life to build upon our inner power, which is and comes from merging, blending into our Original Self.

- *This* then becomes who we are, in the world.

And once you do that, there are no more questions. Because once you do that, all is clear to you. You see all. And you *know, "This is who I Am. This is why I am here. This is why we are all here."*

In this, you are living in grace. In this, you are becoming grace.

That is who you are, dear friend. You *are* the *Light* of grace.

For grace *is* Divine Love, in action.

When you are able to do this, dearest one, that is when you know: who you are, why you are here, and what to do next.

I am your beloved, with you always. In grace, I am your befriender—in *all* that you do.

Once Jesus, a boy, I grew into a man. Now eternally the *Light* of the Original Self, I am forever Sananda.

Blessed be.

Received May 3, 2019

69

The Spectrum

Humanity Is Rays of Light

Hello, dearest ones. All the angels in Heaven are rejoicing. For you are awakening to your true purpose in life: to be a beacon of hope, that others may be glad in their lives.

The world is transforming. And all upon it. The Earth is transforming, as are all humans.

Life as you have known it for millions of years is now shifting into a higher vibratory frequency.

This means that all peoples, in all lands, are now being imbued with a new way of seeing life—as a spectrum.

Life is a rainbow of variations in peoples, in animals, in birds, in plants.

Nurture this *spectrum*. For it is your strength as a species. Nurture this spectrum of hopes, dreams, and creations.

Life is not a place to escape from all around you. It is a place to immerse yourself, so that you fully feel the vibrancy of the world you are in.

Do not shun the world. Embrace the world—the peoples. For you are one of these. And every one of you is a part of the spectrum called humanity.

Humanity is not individuals seeking their own personal gains. Humanity is a composite. You are rays of *Light,* together shaping a whole spectrum of possibilities.

Live not for sustenance as the goal. Live to be sustaining. Live to be your ideal Self, through your insights.

For it is your personal ideas that are your ray of *Light* into the world. It is your personal viewpoints that shine values into the world. It is your personal values that are your voice in the world.

The world is not separate from you. It is the extension of your feelings. It is the expression of your thoughts.

Think *cooperation* and that is the world that shapes around you. Think *understanding* and that is the experiences you shape in your life.

Life is not a separate thing that happens by chance. Life is not a cruel joke that has its own plan.

Life is how you learn to trust yourself.

In your life experiences—especially choices—you learn to choose what inspires you and lifts you up. You learn to be bold, and to lift others up.

Life is where you learn your place in the whole—and *why* it matters what you *think* even more than what you say.

First come ideas. These are the fuel of your imagination.

Second come thoughts: personal ambitions, needs, and wishes. *These* shape your beliefs, your worldviews. Your personal thoughts give rise to your ideologies.

So, for a healthy worldview:

- Live in hope — not fear.
- Live in courage — not confrontation.
- Challenge yourself — not others.
- Re-teach yourself — rather than judge others.
- Be the person you want others to be . . . and these are the people you will draw to you.

Life is not isolation. Life is a spectrum of vibrant choices.

Lift up your own life by lifting up your voice. Live in serenity, rather than rage, and peace will find you.

Joy is in choosing to live as one of the *spectrum*. For every human is a unique ray of *The Light*. Distinguish not others. Only be a present support.

Your life is unique because *you* are a single ray of *Light* who is one of the *spectrum* of all hopes. These hopes are *The Light* of the world.

Shine your hope—and *you* are lifting yourself and others out of despair. For despair is only the lack of hope, and hope is *The Light* of all life.

Earth is your home. Love her. In this way, you are also loving yourself. Nurture her, and you are nurturing yourself.

Earth, too, is a part of the *spectrum* of all life. The spectrum of life is *all* life forms together as a force of good.

Be the balance you seek. In that is peace.

I am your beloved, once Jesus of Nazareth, now eternally Sananda.

Received May 7, 2019

70

There Once Was a Boy

a Story

Dearest ones, this day we look at how you can retain your perceptions of hope in the face of tragedies.

Yes, physical traumas are the greatest challenge. They test your beliefs in Providence.

But, my dears, I can attest that life is a grand perfection, even with all the losses, sorrows, and troubles.

Yes, watching catastrophes unfold is heart-wrenching, and watching peoples' great sorrow in the midst of others' violent acts is wrenching, because it tears at the core of wanting to believe in everyone, and wanton destruction and murder seem so inexplicable.

Yet I can tell you this: Whatever sorrows are wrought against you or those you love, your own heart is still whole and filled with compassion *because* you do feel the devastating crisis impacting lives.

My dearest, keep your heart open. The way to tread through these events is to keep your heart free of bias. Remain in love for the troubled.

Let me tell a story.

> There once was a boy who loved his family, even though they discarded him.
>
> He was very young when he was torn from his mother's arms and given to uncaring wards who kicked him and burned him.
>
> He was treated like garbage, like a wastrel, even though he was a child and had no power. All he could was accept his fate.
>
> But the cruelty fed him. And his lost family haunted him.
>
> He grew in disdain of everyone. Everyone had thrown him around as if they owned him.
>
> He grew up with a fierce hatred because no one had ever been kind to him.
>
> Abandoned, unwanted, abused, he had known only disdain for life.

So when he was a man, he carried this disdain for life himself. He was cruel. He killed animals. And then he struck out against women. For they had abandoned him.

This young man was a fighter. He fought everyone. He became a horrible human being, torturing anyone who looked at him with uncertainty.

Then one day, he killed someone. It wrenched at him. It ate at him. Yet he had known nothing else.

So, resigned to the only life he had known, he relinquished all hope.

He killed again.

This young man became a torment in society. He looked on everyone as his enemy. He trusted no one. And he set himself above all.

This young man took a job doing what he was good at. Hurting people.

And this was his life. He lived with only vengeance in him. He lived not for peace. He cared for no one.

Until one day, an animal came to his doorstep. This lost animal sat at his doorstep for many nights, hungry.

This animal slept on his doorstep night after night, hungry.

This lost animal never left the man. A wayward creature just as the man.

A deer.

This lost deer, also abandoned, young, remained on the man's porch, hungry. Day after day.

The man, drunk in his great shadows, only watched—as the deer grew faint, yet did not move.

The man raged inside his house. "Why are you bothering me! Leave me alone!"

The deer remained on the porch. Sleeping, hungry.

Many days passed and the deer was very weak. The deer shut his eyes, his breathing shallow. He fell into a sleep and did not stir.

The man watched. He watched. He paced. He hammered his head with his hands. "Why are you here! Leave me alone!"

The deer slept, not moving.

The next morning, thinking the deer had died, the man opened the door, went out and touched the deer. It had grown very cold. It was not moving.

Perplexed, confused, the man touched the deer, wondering what to do. What was he to do with a dead deer on his doorstep? He looked at the deer.

Then the deer opened its eyes, faintly.

And the man's heart leapt. Still confused, still mired in his bound heart, he picked up the young deer and cradled it in his large arms, and placed it in his large car, and drove it to a veterinary office he had seen.

He carried the limp deer inside to the vet. Everyone stared.

"Somebody! Somebody, help, please! He's dying!"

The vet gave the deer a dropper of water and held the deer with love. The man watched.

The vet tenderly treated the deer with liquid food through a dropper and gave him more water.

The deer's eyes were still shut, his breathing was shallow. He lay limp on the cold metal table.

The man watched in suspense, torn as he watched the creature lie helpless, awaiting his fate.

After many hours, the man, sitting in the corner, while the vet and technicians treated the deer, the animal began to stir.

Everyone stood up and came to the deer's attention. Still very frail, the deer scrambled to get to his feet. But he was weak.

The vet held the deer lovingly and fed it more water through the dropper. The deer hungrily accepted the water.

The man watched in suspense.

The deer then turned his head and looked straight into the man's eyes, for a long minute.

The deer stared into the man's eyes.

The man stared back. Bound in the moment. Feeling . . . something.

Then the deer lay down his head, and he was gone.

And the man's eyes welled with tears.

My dears, every person is meant to be loved. Every person is seeking to be loved. Be kind.

I am your beloved, Jesus-Sananda. *Received May 8, 2019*

71

Upleveling Now in Vibrational Frequency

Hello, dearest ones. We are all now in a shift of consciousness. Every person—man, woman, child—is undergoing a heightened sense of change. And this change is real.

All that you see around you is in flux. All is in growth. All is in expansion.

Even I.

Even you.

We are all made of the particles of *Light*. You. Me. All peoples. All animals. *And* all worlds. Even the universe. Even *all* the universes.

And *Light* is energy. And *Light* is consciousness. And *Light* is life. And *all* of life, in all forms, is *now* in expansion.

Yes, we are eternal, as ourselves. Yes, the universe is expanding. But, now, something else is happening—physically.

As *Light,* as consciousness, *all* is now upleveling into a higher vibrational frequency. That is *all* life.

For humans, this means an evolutionary shift—in the evolving human body and brain, and also in ideas and abilities far beyond original humans.

Humans are now evolving in genetic abilities, and that means also increased capacities for seeing the whole and comprehending the whole.

You, my dear—when you open your heart—are now also in this *shift.*

In addition to physical changes in the newer generations (since 2001), all of you are also now awakening to a higher grasp of how *all* life is a part of a whole consciousness.

For you, this means, heightened understanding of the spectrum of thought, heightened sensitivity to the needs of the whole, heightened love for all life.

You, my dear awakening *Light,* are expanding. Expanding in how you see yourself and others. Expanding in how you evaluate and deduce what is of value and what is not. Expanding in how you contribute to the whole through mental capacities.

Life is always evolving. Now it is shifting into a higher vibratory frequency. *This* is now evolving *all* on Earth: humans, animals, and the planet itself.

Why does it matter to know this?

- To have hope that things really will get better.
- To see your own place in this planetary shift.
- To believe in yourself and the vision you have held within you. For it is true. Your vision of your life is true.

And that is why I am here, now. That is why I have returned, now.

- To reveal what is happening, and why.
- To reveal how to fix the problems, now and in the future.
- To remind you of who you are . . . and how you *can* be the person you know you are.

Bottom line.

- Live not for yourself alone.
- Improve the lives of others.
- Use your mind.
- Use your creative insights.

You are a solver. Solve. Do not stand by and do nothing. People need you. All the people will benefit from *your* imagination and your ideas.

Lift up others by standing in your own truth.

I am your friend, always with you. Call on me. I am there.
Jesus-Sananda.

Received May 10, 2019

72

The Ultrasonic Sound Frequency

Telepathy, Intuition

Hello, dearest ones.

The universal consciousness is the connection we all have with each other. You and I are able to hear each other through this web of *Light* frequencies. It's like we are on the same thread or fabric of communication.

Think of all communication as an invisible field that generates frequencies at different levels. This is a sound *spectrum* just as there is a light spectrum.

Just as there are ultraviolet rays invisible to the human eye, there are sound waves not discernable by the human ear—but *are* discernible by the human brain.

These sound waves are ultrasonic, something like a higher frequency to microwave, for example; or a radio wave, in particular.

All of life is comprised of frequencies. When attuned to the higher sensitivities, you can learn to perceive the mind or mental vibrational waves, which are a form of communication.

So, not only do you hear angels in this way, you also can learn to hear animals in this way, though that may be in images or emotions, not in words. You also may learn to hear people in this way.

Telepathy is ultrasonic sound. It is being able to attune to the frequency. And it is common among some groups of peoples.

Just as some groups of animals listen and communicate at higher frequencies than the human ear—so do some groups of humans. Some humans are born with this higher frequency activated in both the brain and the nervous system. Others learn it.

This is how people like Charol are able to hear me. Thousands of people on the planet are able to hear the higher frequencies—through the brain.

In addition, *all* humans are able to sense and *feel* the vibration of higher beings. Usually, you are feeling angels.

By this same ability, which is a part of the human body's nervous system, you are also able to discern lies from truth.

This is a life-saving feature in the body's nervous system. Think of it as a built-in alarm.

This is also how you can feel danger en route to you, or present before you.

Life is a spectrum, in many ways. The sound spectrum is a universal web of *Light* frequencies. This is how all of the Travelers communicate. This is how you can hear what is beyond the reach of the human ear.

You are built for this. The sound spectrum is a part of and a feature of the human body.

When we say, *Hear us with your heart,* that is a way to bypass the analytical mind and learn to feel—and discern—using your inborn aptitude for *felt* discernment.

I mention this so you realize—you are already doing this. It is called intuition.

So, dearest ones, *feel* the *Divine Presence,* and hear *The Divine* speaking to you.

We *are* with you.

The spectrum of life also includes dimensions of life co-existing—all on spectrums of *Light.* The dimensions are frequencies.

This is how all exists at-once. This is how the eternal self—the consciousness—never dies.

The consciousness is eternal. The you who lives forever—your soul—is what you think of as *awareness,* or is consciousness. And *this* self exists regardless of the dimensional life it inhabits.

Life spectrums co-exist, as layers of reality. One of these spectrums of life is sound.

I hear you. You hear me, or feel me. Across the dimensions. Across the world.

Space-time is not a barrier to thought. And I *am* with you. In *Light.* Through *Light.*

Always your befriender, I am Jesus-Sananda.

Blessed are you when your heart is willing to hear.

Received May 13, 2019

73

The New Humans

Since 1971, 2001

Hello, dearest souls. Today, we look at how humanity is in a physical evolution.

This began in 1971. The many born since then have a greater brain capacity than 99 percent of humans born before 1971. They have an activated dormant gene, which allows them a greater ability to evaluate, foresee, and comprehend complex analytical processes.

This activated gene in the human DNA is also only one of many *now* activating in people born since 2001. This activation gives these persons the abilities of critical thinking, greater longevity, and increased capacity for imagination—which is actually being able to foresee and contemplate new ways of solving problems.

About 30 percent of people born since 1971 have the first activated gene, and about 33 percent of people born since 2001.

Why?

The human genome was always designed to have periodic triggers into increased capacities, mentally *and* physically.

In the past centuries, this was about .05% of persons. In the future, this increases again.

What does this mean for the human body?

It means that an increasing number of the population, globally, are awakening to innate abilities; such as increased longevity, healthier bodies, and abilities to envision, intuit, and perceive ideas and possibilities, naturally.

These are the people who see solutions easily. For example, they are thinkers and inventors. They are healers and teachers. They are scientists and engineers. They are artists, writers, and filmmakers.

You are very likely one of these, if you are drawn to this book. For it is those who are awakening whose hearts are also awakened to new ideas.

If you are not one whose genome is or has been activated out of dormancy (for there is no junk DNA), you are still awakening spiritually.

The soul is eternal. The soul functions through the physical body. The soul is your original body—of *Light.*

Your spirit is your ability to dream, imagine, and hope. You lift up yourself and others through your emotions, which are your spiritual endeavors and insights.

Spiritually, you are—or already have—awakened to a new hope in your life, in how you see yourself and your place in the world.

This spiritual awakening is for everyone on the planet, in their own time. It is the awakening of your core identity, which then begins to remember the essential truths of life, that:

- Every life matters.
- Every person is born in *The Light* and is born of *The Divine.*
- Every creature has a right to life.

Dearest ones, this peek into the now existing physical evolution is to inspire you into realizing that all of life evolves.

You are not stagnant. Your personality can and does grow. Your choices can change.

You have innate abilities, genetically. You also have emerging abilities to perceive more than you ever thought possible.

Your body has innate abilities. Your mind is eternal. Your consciousness is the part of you that is forever.

You are capable of choosing a path in life that is of your higher dreams and wishes.

Life is not to be thrown away. Physical reality is an opportunity to learn your abilities *and* to share them.

- For you are here—in this life, at this time—to be your best, for others.
- You are here to be an example.
- You are here to share your vision.
- You are here to show how goodness is natural.
- You are here to be your best Self.
- You are here to be kind.
- You are here to live for the highest good of all.

Life is to be revered. Life is not an accident. Nature is not an accident.
All of life—in all forms—came out of *The One Great Mind.*

Cherish what you have, and live as one who cherishes life, and your own life will bless you. For what you are—you create.

I am your beloved brother, once Jesus of Nazareth, eternally Sananda.

I am with you, always, in spirit and in the body.

Here me *within*.

Received May 16, 2019

74
The New Thought Leaders

Dearest ones, today let us look at how you are one of the new visionaries.

- You are blessed with insights not before believed.
- You see the whole of all life—as if life were actually a matrix.
- You see the whole of society, and you feel its threads of continuity.
- You see the whole of the planet, and you feel its power points and binding forces that crisscross the earth.
- You see the universe, and feel its presence of life.

Dearest one —
You are a thought leader in this new Era.
You are a purveyor of all that is coming.
You are a seeker, too. But only because your heart sees truth and you wish to awaken the lost souls who suffer terrible grievances for the abuses they have suffered.

Dearest one —
You are a healer.
You bring wonder into the world, and it empowers the people who have lost hope.
You bring surprise into the world, and it stimulates those who have lost sight of change as a good thing.
You bring the gifts of persuasion and tolerance, and this gives peoples a new way of seeing others who are unlike them.

You, my friend, are your own keeper. You keep your thoughts as sacred. You keep your wishes for the world as a responsibility.
As a Keeper, who is awakened in your conscience and your soul, you are not moved to wrong choices. You now already have learned what is harmful in choices and what will benefit. In this way, you are a leader in thought.

You , my friend, are lifting up the downtrodden.
Let this be your platform.
Let this be the stand you take.

For out of this, the less fortunate arise and, from them, the passions of goodwill toward all.

Be not like any other around you.
Be not like the power hungry who give no thought to others.
Be only the self your heart loves.
Be the self who finds joy in being kind and helpful.
This, my friend, is your true Nature.

And for this, I and the Council of Light are grateful. For you—among the Lightbearers shining truth and kindness in the world—are a leader in this new Era.

Change is not swift. But change is assured. And you are one of those bringing transformation to society, by lifting up the downtrodden.

Be the blessing you were born to be.

I am your beloved, once Jesus of Nazareth, now eternally Sananda. I am your friend, in all that you do.

Received May 17, 2019

75

The Next Four Millennia

Hello, dearest ones. Today let us look at how the human race is now in a shift as a species.

Yes, it is true. You are now in the beginning of a change in the body. This is an evolution of the brain.

This is evident in new abilities, such as envisioning solutions that were not before imagined.

It is evident in an increased capacity for goodwill and in more compassion.

It is evident in a greater awareness of what is unseen by most, the etheric kingdoms.

Basically, increasingly, a greater number of people are today being born with these heightened abilities of perception. Not every person and not all at once, but increasingly—over the next four millennia.

How does this affect you? Are you one of these?

If you find yourself believing in a better world, and you are able to envision how that is possible *and* what your part might be, then yes you are a new human. For that is the hallmark of those who are awakening the whole of humanity.

Humanity, even so, is on the verge of this shift—in attitude.

You, my friend, are in this life to lift up others. Not control them. Not damage them.

You are in this life to bring goodness into the conversation, to remind people of what their hearts tell them, which they have ignored, largely.

You are in this life as a voice of compassion for those who cannot speak for themselves.

Yes, it has always been so. But *today* it is critical. For without embracing the good, people cannot find the purpose of life, which is:

Deep joy in the moment.

Thus, you are here to be the joy.
This is your purpose.

I am your beloved, always your friend. Once called Jesus of Nazareth, eternally I am Sananda.

Received May 19, 2019

76

And Now We Are in The Second Days

Dearest humanity, these *are* the days long foretold, the days given by some as the last days.

But, my friends, these are *not* the last days. These are The Second Days.

Humanity has completed The First Days of its plan: to expand, to learn.

In the now Second Days—which is countless millennia—humanity expands in insight and in wisdom.

In these now Second Days of humanity's endless journey, you discover a higher purpose. You rise into a higher peoples, who are more intent on loving than on hurting.

In these now Second Days—humanity's new beginning—you are awakened to your original purpose, which is: *To love one another.*

There is no greater command.

And in this spirit, I too beseech you:

> *Love one another.*
>
> For you are one body, not many. And what you do unto others, you do unto yourself. *Literally.*

I am your beloved, once called the savior of the world.

But, my dears, I am only one of thousands of great Teachers to the human species, on Earth and beyond.

Worship not me, nor any other. We come only to teach what we have learned that you, too, may be free—in your own heart.

Blessed be.

I am eternally Sananda.

Received May 21, 2019

77

The Deep Calming Breath

a Meditation

Dearest ones, your life in this world is an opportunity to express your higher goals, not only for yourself but for all.

This is a world of extremes. Find your center. Live in the center.

This is a world of confusion. Live in clarity. In your center.

This is a world of hardships. Live in compassion. From your center.

What is your center? It is the part of you that is calm, focused, and serene.

How do you find this center? Through the deep calming breath. Let us now practice how to do that.

Meditation

Be in a spot that is yours alone.
Surrender to the moment.
Let go of all that haunts you.

Now find this quiet breath coming into you.
Let it in . . .
gently peacefully filling you . . .
Breathe it in.

Breathe in the waves of serenity . . .
like a calm stream gently laps upon the banks . . .
like a quiet night's breeze gently lulls you into surrender . . .

Sinking into this deep abiding breath.
It is comforting . . .
as you let yourself simply be there . . .
without hurry . . .
without rushing . . .
letting your body lull into this wakeful surrender. . . .

Dearest one, life is your place to find your quiet center.

No matter where you are, life is the path to the inner clarity.

For when you can be *here*—amidst all that is in the world around you—you see clearly and know clearly *how* to be your own solution.

The answers for what to do—in this moment—are in the gentle deep calming breath.

As you learn to be in this surrender to the inner clarity, a calm fills you and the understanding of your life can then come into your awareness.

When you are able to be *here,* you are focused on being. And this is the you who can see what you need to know and can hear what is already around you.

Let this be your process, daily, and you will know the answer to "Who am I? Why am I here?"

For the answers are in your soul.

And you hear and feel your soul in the quiet place, within.

The quiet place is inside you.

I am your beloved. I am with you always, in spirit and in the body.

I am Sananda, once Jesus of Nazareth, forever the right hand of *The Divine Consciousness,* who guides us all.

Received June 8, 2019

78

The Ten Keys

Hello, dearest ones.

The universe is expanding. All of life also is expanding.

Humanity is on the cusp of a life-altering shift in self-awareness. This means that over the next several millennia, many:

- You will be learning the value of seeing ahead—to what you can be.
- You will be learning how to forgive, and to accept.
- You will be learning to reflect and to engage in your better nature.

This is a learned skill for humanity.

Let us say that, as of now, humanity is just leaving childhood. You are not yet in maturity. You are still filled with rancor, at times.

Yes, you are recognizing the need for humility, but this is not yet a trait that comes easily.

Then there are the handful who have acquired this. They are the great spiritual leaders.

Let's look at how they have done this, so that you can see how you also can do this because you are no different.

- Believe in your better nature, and hone it.
- Believe in humanity's better nature, and fill your days with helping that to become so.
- Live each moment in an attitude of at-one-ment with all of life. Revere life, in all of its forms. This teaches humility.
- Forgive yourself of your mistakes and of any harm you have caused.
- Forgive others of any harm they have caused. These two steps teach humility.
- Listen to the inner counsel for guidance in your days, which is the loving clarity of choices that help you and also are in the highest good of others. This teaches humility.
- Practice daily a meditation, to attune your mind and emotions to a higher acceptance. This relieves anger and fear.

- Practice daily a deep breathing routine, to retrain your body and your thoughts. This restores physical focus and also strengthens resistance to disease.
- Live in a daily intention to be helpful. This teaches humility.
- Live in a daily practice to be open and honest. This teaches humility.

The higher thoughts are a practiced routine. Be this higher person, living in your best goals and intentions, each day, and you will train yourself to think and feel as your higher Nature.

Being in your higher Nature is, for most, a learned skill.— But it *is* already in you.

Yes, a few display these traits exceptionally well. They also practice the intention and the effort *every* day, to freshen the innate responses.

Humility and wisdom are learned. Practice—daily—what you wish to be.

I am your beloved, once Jesus of Nazareth, eternally Sananda.

Received June 9, 2019

79

I Call Every Girl and Every Boy

Hello, dearest ones.

Today, let us talk about how your life is one of a kind. You are not like anyone else.

This is why I am speaking personally to you, now. Because I need your help.

Dearest one, I need your faith. I need your power of convictions.

Today, humanity is striving to be the full Intention: to live as one in hope and in conscience.

Also, today, the planet is choking.

Also, today, the animals are dying.

Dearest one, you are my helper in this world. You are compassionate. You care what happens to the animals. You care what happens to the earth, the seas, the air. You know that humanity is plagued with suffering.

This is why *you* can help.

Your own vision is one of the solutions. Your own sensitivity and grand proposals are a part of the healing of hearts and minds—through which the healing comes for the planet and the societies.

Dearest one, it is not by chance that you found me in this book. It is not by chance that you find me on this day.

You are my helper, as a voice of persuasion in the world. You are my helper, as a teacher of thoughtful grace. You are my helper, as a passionate girl or woman, boy or man.

You, my dearest, are a healer of this world. It requires persistence to reach the many. It requires courage to lift yourself up out of your circumstances.

But, my dearest, that is who you are. You have in you the wisdom of the angel you once were. You also have in you the strength of the angels who lift *you* up today—as they do for the many who are afraid of life, the many who are tortured or enslaved, the many who are forgotten or ignored.

This, my dearest, is where the need is great.

You are *where* you are to help those around you, your family, your community.

Feel my presence in your heart. Feel the help of the angels in every day.

Now expand your dreams. For *this* is why you are here. Now.

You are in *this* life, at *this* time, to be the fullest Self you already are.

You were born to this.

So, lift up the hopes of all around you. Lift up those who are poor. Lift up those who are hungry. Lift up those who are sick.

This is your calling.

And in this, I am with you—I and all the Masters of Wisdom, I and all the angels of all the dimensions.

You are on the Earth, in *this* life, to help all around you.

For life is not meant to be a burden. And you can help to renew and grow the Original Intention for humanity: to live as one, in hopes, in peace, in conscience, and in joy.

For this, you are a blessing in the world.

And for this, your own life will be easier than it has been.

For when you live in your strength, you know who you are.

You are an angel, remembering.

As are all.

I am your beloved, with you always, in spirit and in the body. I am Jesus-Sananda.

Received June 10, 2019

80

A Current of Hope Is Sweeping Across Every Land

On this day, beloved, you are in concert with the whole. Therefore, choose your thoughts carefully. Live in integrity. Live in empathy.

For this is a day when an increase in awareness is breaking through the dull hearts. An increase in sympathizing is arising in the angry. And an increase in defiance is pouring out of the mouths of the distressed.

This is a day of more awareness, for more people, than ever before on the Earth. A day of disgust with cruelty, by more hearts than ever before on the Earth. A day of sadness at intolerance, by more minds than ever before in human history.

Dearest one, therefore, on this day let your thoughts be to open your own heart and to open your own life to a greater service.

For you were born in *this* life, at *this* time, to be a teacher in truth and a leader in kindness.

- For only truth and kindness can heal souls of disparity.
- Only truth and kindness can heal hardened hearts and dulled minds.
- Only truth and kindness can awaken the destitute to their own power: to live free.

This, my dear, is your destiny: to open hearts to kindness.

- Judge not the destitute. For they are you.
- Judge not the tortured. For they are you.
- Judge not yourself. For you also are in concert with all whom you see around you.

This is a day to be still—in thought—so that you may *feel* the whole of humanity. In this way, you *feel* the current of hope sweeping across every land.

This is your calling: to raise hope in the hearts of all you know.

In this way, you are a bearer of goodness. And a bearer of tenderness.

In this way, tread softly. But surely. Live with a strength of purpose: to lift up all you see, so that everyone will come to feel the peace of their own higher purpose. Because when we live our higher purpose, that is when we are fully aligned in God.

I am your beloved, once Jesus of Nazareth, eternally Sananda. With you in every hour. With you in spirit and in body.

You are my blessed brother.

You are my kindred sister.

In God, we are one.

Received June 17, 2019

81

These Days Toward Awakening

This is the day.

On this day, *The Light* of God is opening a window of insight in the hearts of the multitudes.

On this day, the heart of God is opening a window of truth in the minds of the multitudes.

On this day, *The Light* of God is opening a window of courage in the spirits of the multitudes.

For it is courage that helps you to stand up for what is right for the greater good.

It is courage that is your own Higher Self living in you.

It is courage that is the vibrant Self you already are and were born to be—in *this* life.

Lift up in the courage of your inner wisdom. Lift up in the inner strength of what is right for all.

For these are the days toward change. These are the days toward the awakening of the many to seeing that this world *is* for all.

Every person is innately good.

Every person was born in *Light*.

Every person seeks *Light* . . . and eventually will restore the *Light* within.

Acceptance is the key to peace of mind and peace with others.

Acceptance is recognizing the inborn *Light* in every other—and in yourself. For you already know it.

Now allow it. So that you may, at last, be what you were born to be: your full Self . . . in the world:

Gracious. Tender. Wise.
Listening within. Hearing within.

For this is the day—to be your full Self, and not for yourself alone.

For a full heart is one that is open to others.

A full heart gives *Light* to all around it.
A full heart is yours when you, humbly and at long last, accept:

> *This* is my *Light*.
> I *am* my *Light*.
> And my *Light* is all I am and all I wish to be.
> For my *Light* is who I really am, who I wish to be, and who I can be.
> As are we all.

And so it is.
Yours eternally, Jesus-Sananda.

Received June 19, 2019

82

This New Era of Grace

Dearest souls, on *this* day, all of humanity are in a moment of grace.
Despite the sorrows, hardships and anger, every one of you is not judged.
Not one of you is spiritually held in contempt.
Not one of you is spiritually strangled for your miscreant behaviors.
Not one of you is spiritually restricted due to your attitudes.

This is an Era of grace. Because all of humanity are going through a cleansing.

In the hardships, you are being thrust into situations that require stamina of spirit and stamina of mind.

In the hardships, you are being reconstructed—from within—in how you value life and others.

In the hardships, you are being recalibrated in how you see yourself—and others.

Sorrow is a healer. Sorrow is a mirror.

- See yourself in others' actions. — Do not judge.
- See yourself in others' failures. — Do not see others as less, only as troubled.
- See the despair in the world—*and* see the goodwill seeded in it.

For despair is a motivator.

Despair pushes you to lift yourself up out of the muck of futility with your circumstances and to find your way into your calm center.

Despair is not futility. Despair is an engine, within which to fire up your grievances and push through them.

Today, let go of sorrow and despair—by leaning into the challenges to your heart.

Give in to nothing. Stand up and keep going.

You are here to live fully and brightly. Your *Light* is a strength of courage and an aptitude for survival.

Do not give in to your uncertainties. Push through them.
For you are not your despair amidst circumstances.
You are the *Light* that can shine so brightly that nothing else will be seen.

You are the *Light* that shines so fervently that shadows shrink, and only hope remains.

On this day, trust your inner calm—which is your center of truth:

> In *The Light,* all is clear.
>
> In *The Light,* all is clarified.
>
> In *The Light* is your answer and your vision.
>
> In *The Light* is born how to be in the world—and how to be in your own fully evolved spiritual Nature, wherein all is clarified, wherein all becomes clear.

I am your beloved, Jesus-Sananda. And I am with you always, in spirit and in the body.

Received June 22, 2019

83
Epilogue

And so on this day, my dearest friends, I end this current series. I will write again.

I do have other materials I am now sharing through Charol. After a while, I will bring you more of these Letters as well.

I wish you the full heart that I see in you.

Never forget, I *am* in your life, today. I *am* in the world, with you—I and all the saints, the Teachers and Masters of all the Ages on Earth, I and the multitude of the angels.

We are with you as teachers and guides. We are with you as healers and protectors. We are with you in all forms of presence as love.

For of all the qualities that most represent you—and represent us—is love.

Let us never forget. We *are* love, and that is *The Light* of God.

Love *is* the heart of God.

And, in love, I am always in your presence.

Jesus-Sananda. Always.

Received June 23, 2019

84

Lastly, a Deep Calming Breath

a Meditation

Take a deep breath.... Let it out slowly.
Allow your mind and feelings to slow down.
Feel yourself calm and in a deep stillness.

Here, feel your core essence,
a quiet peaceful presence where only contentment holds you.

In this peaceful center, feel and see
a gentle *Light* from your center and all around you.
Be in this gentle *Light,* allowing awareness to fill you.

When you are ready, open your eyes
and feel the deep calm in you.
Live in it today. Live in it as you work and play.
Live in it as you sleep, lulled in a deep calm,
wherein you know who you are and why you are here.

This is your true self,
always present, always serene,
always clear and at peace,
always assured in your place today in your life.

In this, you know
how to be in this moment and let all else go.
In this, you know
how to embrace the true you and live it today in the world.

Remember, this is who you are.
And it is already in you.
All you need to do is be still,
and go in with the calming breath.

Blessed are those whose hearts are kind.
Blessed are those whose words are kind.
Blessed are those who walk in humility.
Blessed are those who wait with patience.
Blessed are those who listen, and who hear, and chastise not.

Appendices

Jesus Here How Long?

June 9, 2019

"How long have you been here?" I asked Jesus, after writing for the day.

With a smile in his voice, he answered, "For your entire lifetime."

"So at least since July 14, 1945?"

"Before the War."

"Before World War II?"

"Yes."

January 27, 2019

"Charol, it was me all along, from the beginning," he told me. "I am your Master Teacher. It's been me writing to you all these decades as the I AM and the Universal Consciousness. I've been behind everything you've been writing."

September 30, 2019

As I was listening to the Audible version of this book, with a male narrator as Jesus, and feeling as if I were sitting at Jesus' feet among a few close disciples, he said to me, "Democracy survives."

February 17, 2021, 2:30 pm MT

"This is only the beginning for America."

The Messenger's Awakening

The Divine Presence exuded through every cell of my being, nurturing every thought, attitude, and emotion. I had come out of a long inner darkness and a month of unexpected awakened intuitive abilities.

It was Sunday, November 2, 1975, two a.m. I was thirty years old, divorced, and living alone in my apartment in Colorado Springs, Colorado.

In the middle of this long dark night, a spontaneous mystical activation into cosmic consciousness shattered my self-image and transformed my sense of self, as if I had been picked up and set in the opposite direction.

My outpouring heart opened me to all the wisdom of the ages streaming into my consciousness. I poured myself wholly into the fullness of this new divine and ecstatic place of human beingness, and a tremendous euphoria filled me. I felt the grandeur of the Universal Consciousness—of which I then *knew* I was an integral part. For the first time, I had a sense of identity and a sense of purpose.

An irrepressible explosion of insight and wisdom whirled through me, transforming my small sense of self into something profound and larger. The world was suddenly filled with vibrant sounds, textures, images, and colors. Extraordinary grace expanded my imagination, hopes and desires, surpassing anything I had ever thought possible for my life. For the first time, I truly was stepping into, onto the edge of my future, my destiny.

Doubt succumbed to hope, possibility, potential, and all the extraordinary dreams that would keep me stretching. The shackles and blinders of my previous existence fell away and I saw my true life, the true world, and the true destiny of humanity and of each soul.

I saw the lights of every soul on earth. I saw us all transcending our small narrow lives, lifting up into our true light, our true nature. I saw who we really are: We are large. We are a grand species. We are individuals filled with the ideal Self.

It was in this revelatory moment, the culmination of many days of out-of-body visions and transcendent travels, that I knew why I was in this life, this world, this body.

The very next breath I took was the first breath of my new life. I breathed for the first time with the fullness of Spirit, with the heart of a gentle and valiant soul, with the mind of a seer and a teacher of wisdom, to remind us all who we really are. For we have always been this grand Self. None of us has ever stopped being this grand Self.

In this moment of my first breath, I saw the wholeness of us all. I saw our glad hearts. I saw and felt the smiles and laughter of our true Nature. I felt the yearning of our hearts for release from pain and anguish. I felt the cries of our true beings for peace and sanity. I felt the pull of all souls in the world to find a way to be reminded of their inner light, to find a way to rekindle that connection, to find a way to remember and once again live from that place of our deep Self that is sacred and free of all regret.

In that moment, Spirit set itself upon me. Spirit opened my heart, my mind, my eyes, my ears, my tongue; giving me gifts of knowing, knowledge of the inner worlds, knowledge of our true Selves, knowledge and understanding of what we are and what we once again can be, knowledge of where we are evolving as a people, knowledge of how to help individuals remember.

In this hour of awakening to my true Self, my destiny came upon me as a cloak of surrender, no matter what the cost; a cloak of sanctity to give all that I am to help the people of this world find even a moment or a glimpse of what I *knew* in this single hour.

Since that day, I have had many hours, at times many months, of uninterrupted bliss and a continuous glow in the rapture of the Divine Presence breathing its force through me, that I may fulfill my purpose—which is to rekindle the *memory* of what we all are: divine beings.

That tremendous surging Vital Force still pushes me to transcend my everyday reality and to continue to reach out—because that is how we grow, that is how we each have made it this far, how we always have evolved and become more as a people and as individuals.

Awakened to my divine Nature, the fullness of Spirit flooded my being, flushed, purged, and nurtured my every thought and feeling to be a voice of the Divine, a hand of the Divine, to share with others whatever the Divine gives through me.

Graced by the splendid touch of God, thereafter transformed, I gave over my life wholly to be of service. That was the beginning of my life and the opening of my journey into my heart.

The Messenger Books

THE BRINGERS OF HOPE: In Jesus' Words, Today - Expanded Second Edition 2021. The New Jesus Chronicles, Book 3 (2021).

YOUR AWAKENING ATTITUDE OF SERVICE: In Jesus' Words, Today – on The Fifth Level of Consciousness. *Four awards:* 2021, First Place Winner in both the categories Inspiration and Spirituality with Firebird Book Awards, as well as Third Place Winner in Personal Growth; and 2021 International Second Place Winner, Book Excellence Awards in Inspirational. The New Jesus Chronicles, Book 2 (2020).

IN JESUS' WORDS, TODAY: Humanity's Magnificent Future – Prestigious Kairos Crystal Award 2019, and two TV interviews, with Preach the Word Worldwide Network. The New Jesus Chronicles, Book 1 (2019, First Edition).

THE NEW HUMANS: Second Genesis – International First Place Winner in Soul Bridge Book Awards of Europe in The Spiritual Awakening of Humanity, 2017; and International Second Place Winner, Book Excellence Awards in Body-Mind-Spirit, 2017. Second Edition 2018. Series "*The New Humanity*" Book 3.

HUMANITY 2.0: The New Humanity – *Five awards* include: Honorary Shining Stars Crystal Award, 2019, plus TV interview, with Preach the Word Worldwide Network; International Second Place Winner, Book Excellence Awards in Spirituality, 2019. Second Edition 2018. Series "*The New Humanity*" Book 2. (Book 1 *The New Humanity,* 2000, first edition, written 1994)

YOU 2.0: Living Your Infinite Self – International First Place Winner, Book Excellence Awards in Personal Growth, 2016. Second Edition 2018.

THE SOUL PATH – National Finalist USA Best Books in General Spirituality, 2015. 2018 3rd Ed.

INTUITION FOR EVERY DAY, a spirituality everyday workbook, dozens of personal anecdotes on Charol's mystical experiences – National Finalist USA Best Books New Age Nonfiction, 2015. 2018 2nd Ed.

WINGS OF LIGHT: The Four Angels Who Guide You – National Finalist CIPA EVVY in Spirituality, 2012. 2018 2nd Ed.

THE POWER OF COURAGE: An Uplifting Saga of Moving Beyond Abuse — Second Place Winner international Book Excellence Awards in New Nonfiction, 2016; and National Finalist USA Best Books in Women's Issues, 2015 (expanded third edition in development, retitled *Finding My Power and Courage,* narrative nonfiction memoir).

I'M DANCING AS FAST AS I CAN – National Finalist USA Best Books, memoir, 2005.

A messenger of her oversoul and the first angel clan and master Jesus, since her spontaneous Higher Self awakening in 1975, Charol Messenger was also certified as a clear channel of Ascended Masters and the Spiritual Hierarchy in 1983 through The Tibetan Foundation. In the 1980s, Charol founded the Books for Iraq charity, shipping books on all topics to troops and Iraqi children. She published the international newsletter *Global Citizen* 1987-88. She has a B.A. in English, philosophy, and world religions from the University of Colorado, 1985.

Printed in Great Britain
by Amazon

73665151R00144